Blanche Knott's
TREASURY
OF
TASTELESSNESS

Blanche Knott's
TREASURY
OF
TASTELESSNESS

BLANCHE KNOTT

ST. MARTIN'S PRESS
New York

ISBN 0-312-11343-9

First Edition: November 1994

10 9 8 7 6 5 4 3 2 1

For TLD again;
he deserves it.

CONTENTS

Blanche Knott's

TREASURY
OF
TASTELESSNESS

ETHNIC VARIEGATED

Did you hear about the man who was half Polish and half Italian?
He made himself an offer he couldn't understand.

* * *

Why did the Mafia have Einstein killed?
He knew too much.

* * *

An American, a Russian, an Iraqi, and an Israeli were walking down the street when a man came up to them and said, "Excuse me. I'm with the Gallup Organization and we're conducting a public-opinion poll about the meat shortage—"

The Russian said, "What's meat?"
The American said, "What's a shortage?"
The Iraqi said, "What's public opinion?"
And the Israeli said, "What's excuse me?"

* * *

Did you hear about the German-Chinese restaurant?
An hour after you eat, you're hungry for power.

* * *

Luigi and Marco had been friends since kindergarten, and remained inseparable throughout their childhood. And when Luigi finally decided to get married, the old friends decided to make a night of it.

At the reception the booze flowed like water, the band played on, and it was well past midnight when Luigi realized he hadn't seen his wife or Marco for quite some time. Staggering around, he finally found his bride and his best friend energetically screwing on a couch upstairs. The groom gazed at the oblivious couple for a few moments, and then burst into laughter so hysterical that the noise brought several members of his family running.

Taking in the scene, his father asked, "What the hell's so goddamn funny?"

"That Marco," said Luigi, wiping the tears of laughter off his cheeks, "he's so drunk he thinks he's me."

* * *

Why don't blacks mug Jews on Yom Kippur?

They fast.

* * *

How can you tell if an Italian is in the Mafia?

His favorite dish is broken leg of lamb.

* * *

Things got so tight for Fernandez that the petty thief turned to armed robbery. "Stick 'em up!" he ordered a burly fellow one dark night.

"You're barking up the wrong tree, pal," said his victim mildly. "This recession is so bad I haven't had more than five bucks in my pocket for a week now."

"You think *that's* hard times?" protested Fernandez bitterly. "See this gun? I haven't been able to afford any bullets for a month."

* * *

What does an Asian person use for a blindfold?

Dental floss.

* * *

What's a Mexican cannibal's favorite food?

Refried beings.

* * *

Deciding it was time for a history review, the teacher asked the class, "Who can tell me what historical figure said, 'I have not yet begun to fight'?"

The little Japanese girl in the front row raised her hand and answered, "John Paul Jones."

"Very good, Miyako. Now, who can tell me who said, 'I regret that I have but one life to give for my country'?"

Again the little Japanese girl was the only one to raise her hand, and piped up, "That's Nathan Hale."

The teacher said to the class, "What's going on? So far Miyako's the only one to answer any of my questions."

2

Suddenly a voice was heard from the back of the room. "Aw, fuck the Japanese!"

"Who said that?" asked the teacher sharply.

Miyako's hand shot up. "Lee Iacocca!"

* * *

Why didn't the African-American want to marry a Mexican?

He didn't want the kids to be too lazy to steal.

* * *

Did you hear about the Scotsman who was so cheap that he went out into the yard on Christmas Eve and fired a shotgun?

He wanted to tell his kids that Santa had killed himself.

* * *

Did you hear about the enterprising Puerto Rican who made a fortune?

He sold maternity first-communion dresses.

* * *

It was just before a critical offensive, and the Polish troops were being issued their weapons. Lenski was last in line, and they handed out the last rifle to the man in front of him. Furious, Lenski shouted, "Hey, what about my gun?"

"Listen, bud," advised the munitions officer, "just keep your hands out in front of you as though you were holding one, and yell, 'Bang! Bang!' "

"You gotta be joking," blustered Lenski. "You must be trying to get me killed!"

"Trust me," said the officer, sending Lenski out into the field with a reassuring pat on the shoulder.

Pretty soon Lenski found himself in the thick of battle with a Russian infantryman advancing on him. Having little choice, he raised his hands, pointed at the soldier, and yelled, "Bang! Bang!" The Russian fell over, stone dead. This worked on about twenty Russians. Fired with confidence, Lenski returned to the munitions officer and asked about a bayonet.

"Oh, we're all out," said the officer apologetically, "but if you just point with your index finger and scream, 'Stab! Stab!' you'll get excellent results."

Out went Lenski into battle again, and soon he was surrounded by heaps of dead Russian soldiers. In fact, he thought he had wiped out the whole platoon, and was just taking a breather when he saw a giant Russian coming towards him. Strutting forward, Lenski shouted, "Bang! Bang!"

The Russian kept on coming.

"Stab! Stab!" cried Lenski.

The Russian kept on coming, right over Lenski, crushing him to a pulp. The last thing the unfortunate Pole heard was the Russian muttering, "Tank, tank, tank. . . . "

* * *

Why did God create armadillos?

So Mexicans would have something to eat on the half shell.

* * *

A Russian, a Jamaican, an American, and a Mexican were on a rafting expedition together. Mid-river the Russian pulled out a *huge* bottle of Stolychnaya, took a swig, and threw it overboard.

"Hey, what the hell d'you do that for?" blurted the American.

"We have so much vodka in Russia that we can afford to waste it," explained the Russian cheerfully.

A few miles downstream the Jamaican took out a *huge* bag full of marijuana, rolled a giant joint, took a few puffs, and tossed it overboard.

"Jesus, that stuff's expensive," howled the American. "What'd you do that for?"

"In Jamaica, weed grows everywhere, mon," said the Jamaican with a grin. "We can afford to waste it."

Thinking hard, the American settled back into his seat. A few miles downriver he stood up with a smile and threw the Mexican overboard.

* * *

Hear about the guy who was half Jewish and half Japanese?

He was circumcised at Benny Hannah's.

* * *

What do you call a Mexican hooker who doesn't bother to charge for her services?

A free-holey.

* * *

Did you hear about the Ku Klux Klansman who had a bed-wetting problem?

He went to rallies in a rubber sheet.

* * *

Garcia was recruited off the street to be in a police lineup on a rape case. When the police brought in the victim, Garcia spoke right up. "Yeah, that's her!"

* * *

What's red, green, blue, purple, and yellow?

An Italian all dressed up.

* * *

The Goldsteins were deeply committed to various social issues, and realized that the best way they could help the homeless would be to take a disadvantaged person into their home. Off they went to a city shelter, where they picked a destitute young black woman, and brought her home. For a very generous salary, the girl was supposed to cook and do light housework, and though she proved both lazy and inept, the couple kept her on.

Shawnette had been with them over a year when she came into the living room one evening and announced that she was pregnant.

The Goldsteins' faces fell. "How did it happen, Shawnette?" asked Mrs. Goldstein gently.

She shrugged. "Beats me." And she went back to her room to watch television.

After talking it over, the couple realized they couldn't put the girl back in the street in her time of need. In fact, they not only kept her on, they adopted the child to spare her any embarrassment.

Nine months later, again without any apology or explanation, Shawnette announced she was pregnant again. Again the Goldsteins loyally kept her on and adopted the child, though it meant moving to a larger apartment.

Six months after that, Shawnette informed them, "I'm gonna have another baby."

"We're not happy about this, Shawnette," said Mr. Goldstein sternly. "Your behavior isn't exactly responsible. But of course we'll adopt this one, too."

"That's not all," said the girl, as surly as ever. "I'm quittin'."

5

"Quitting!" The couple was shocked. "How can you consider such a thing?"

"I agreed to do some cookin' and cleanin'," Shawnette pointed out, "but you never said nothin' 'bout workin' for a family with three kids."

* * *

How do you get forty Haitians in a shoe box?

Tell them it floats.

* * *

How do you stop five blacks in the middle of a rape?

Throw 'em a basketball.

* * *

The sheriff arrived at the scene of the horrible accident just as his deputy was climbing down from the controls of a bulldozer. "Say, Junior, what's going on?" he asked.

"Whole bus full of migrant workers went out of control and over the cliff. I just got through burying 'em," explained the deputy.

"Good work, boy," said the sheriff. "Pretty gory work. Were all of them dead?"

Junior nodded gravely. "Some of 'em said they weren't, but you know how those Mexicans lie."

* * *

What do you get when you cross a Pole and a Chicano?

A kid who spray-paints his name on chain-link fences.

* * *

How do you sink an Irish submarine?

Knock on the door.

* * *

A Pole, an Italian, and an Irishman planned an expedition across the Sahara, and at the appointed time each showed up with his supplies. Motioning to his flask, the Irishman pointed out, "It's going to be a thirsty business, this crossing the desert, and I'll need a drop to drink."

Nodding his approval, the Italian held up a potful of pasta. "I'm gonna get hungry out there."

They looked across to the Pole, who was carrying nothing but a turquoise-and-white left front door of a '57 Chevy. "It's going to be plenty hot," he explained, "and I want to be able to roll down the window."

* * *

How can you spot a Jewish Ethiopian?

He's the one with the Rolex around his waist.

* * *

What do you call a pitiful Puerto Rican?

Despicable.

* * *

An Irishman got engaged to a lovely Lithuanian girl. When they went in for their blood tests it quickly became apparent to the doctor that the husband-to-be had no idea what sexual intercourse consisted of. Taking pity on the bride, Dr. Jones explained about the birds and the bees and the coconut trees, but the vague smile on the young man's face was unconvincing. The doctor's second attempt to explain the ritual of the wedding night left the Irishman smiling and nodding but clearly baffled. The good physician gave it one more try, to no avail.

Thoroughly frustrated, the doctor instructed the young woman to undress and to lie down upon the examination table. She obeyed happily enough, and Dr. Jones, a humanitarian through and through, proceeded to demonstrate for the Irishman. For forty minutes he demonstrated. Finally, sweaty and exhausted, he hauled himself up on his elbows, turned to the fiancé, and said, "*Now* do you understand what I've been trying to tell you?"

At last a glimmer of comprehension came into the Irishman's blue eyes. "I've got it now, Doc," he cried happily.

"Good, good," said the doctor in relief, getting down from the table and pulling up his pants. "Do you have any further questions?"

"Just one," admitted the young man.

"Yes?" asked the doctor testily.

"All I need to know, Dr. Jones, is how often do I have to bring her in?"

* * *

How can you tell when you're flying Vatican Airlines?

The emergency instructions are in Latin so good Catholics can get out first.

* * *

What do you get when you cross a Jew and a Puerto Rican?

A superintendent who thinks he owns the building.

* * *

The Secretary of State came into the Oval Office with a long face. "I'm afraid I've got some bad news, Bill," he said to the president, "but I've got some good news, too."

"Give me the bad news first," instructed Clinton.

"Fifty Japanese tourists were just kidnapped in broad daylight in front of the Hyatt Regency Hotel."

"Jesus," said Clinton with a gasp. "What's the good news?"

"We have forty-three thousand pictures of the terrorists."

* * *

What do Japanese men do when they have erections?

Vote.

* * *

There was once a mobster who employed a deaf-and-dumb accountant. He was satisfied until the year he decided to double-check the books and found that he was short two million dollars; so he sent out a couple of goons to bring the guy in to his office. An hour or so later the cowering accountant arrived, accompanied by a brother who could speak sign language. "You tell that son of a bitch I want to know where my two million bucks is at," boomed the mobster.

After a quick exchange, the translator reported that his brother knew nothing about it.

The boss stood up, pulled out a gun, and came around the desk to hold it against the accountant's neck. "You tell this son of a bitch that if he doesn't tell me where the dough is, I'm going to blow his brains out—after I have the boys work him over."

This was duly translated to the quaking accountant, who gestured frantically to his brother that the money was stashed in three shoeboxes in his closet.

"So whaddid he say?" interrupted the gangster impatiently.

The translator turned and replied, "He says you haven't got the balls to blow his brains out."

* * *

How can you tell where Amish people live in Appalachia?

They have a dead horse up on blocks in the front yard.

* * *

The sophisticated New Yorker was vacationing in the Allegheny mountains when he lost control of his Mercedes. The car plunged off the winding road and over a steep cliff, but Stein managed to roll out and grab hold of a root at the very top of the cliff. There he clung, screaming for help, until a comely young hillbilly came to the edge of the cliff and looked down on his white knuckles and panicked face.

"Please help me," he pleaded.

"There ain't nuthin' in it fer me," she pointed out laconically, hands on her hips.

"I'll do anything, anything you want, just give me a hand," begged Stein.

"Will you suck my titties?" she asked.

"Sure, absolutely," he agreed.

"How about lickin' me all over?"

"You bet."

"And then would you tongue my pussy for hours and hours?" the hillbilly pressed.

"I'd love to," gasped Stein frantically.

"You filthy pervert!" And she stomped on his fingers.

* * *

Did you hear about the Mexican who had a heart attack on Halloween?

Someone came to his door dressed as a job.

* * *

How about Evil Knievel's latest stunt?

He's going to run across Somalia with a sandwich tied to his back.

* * *

Hersch was a salesman. One day as he was driving across the Negev desert he spotted what looked like a body by the side of the road. Hersch slammed on the brakes, ran over, and discovered an Arab on the brink of death. Hersch took the poor man into his arms and bent close so he could make out his parched whisper.

"Water, effendi . . . water."

"Are you in luck!" cried Hersch exultantly. "Why right here in my carrying case, which I happen to have right here beside me, I happen to have the finest collection of one hundred per cent silk neckties to be found this side of the King David Hotel. Normally thirty-five dollars, but for you, twenty-two fifty."

"Water, effendi, water," gasped the Arab, plucking feebly at Hersch's sleeve.

"I tell you what. Since you seem like such a nice guy, I'll make it two for thirty-five—that's for a poly-silk blend, though, I gotta tell you."

"Water, effendi, water."

"You drive a hard bargain." Hersch shook his head regretfully. "Okay, any tie you want for sixteen fifty—but I can't go any lower."

"Water, effendi, water." The dying Arab's words were barely audible.

"Oh, it's *water* you want. Why didn't you say so?" Hersch's voice was filled with reproach. "Well, you're in luck again. Just over that sand dune's a lovely resort; I used to vacation there myself. They'll have all the water you can drink." And Hersch got back in his car and drove away.

The Arab managed to stagger to the top of the sand dune, and, sure enough, a neon-lit sign announcing Le Club Gaza could be seen from the top. The Arab summoned the last of his strength, crawled across the burning sand to the entrance, and collapsed. "Water, effendi. Water," he croaked.

"Ah, you want water," said the doorman sympathetically. "We have all kinds: mineral water, well water, Evian, club soda, Perrier, seltzer. Only thing is, you have to have a tie to get in."

* * *

What do they call "Hee Haw" in Oklahoma?

A documentary.

* * *

What do you get when you cross a Chinese person and a hooker?

Someone who'll suck your laundry clean.

* * *

The Eastern Bloc family was visited by a Western friend, who found only the young daughter at home. "When will your father be back?" he inquired.

"In sixteen hours, eight minutes, and twenty-seven seconds," the little girl replied crisply.

"My goodness—where is he?"

"He is in his twenty-sixth orbit around the Earth."

"I see." The visitor was clearly impressed. "And your mother, when will she be home?"

The little girl shrugged.

"Can you give me some idea when she's expected?"

The little girl shook her head.

"Come on now," said the visitor, persistently. "How is it that you know to the second when your father will be back from outer space but can't even manage a guess as to when I can see your mother? Where is she?"

"She's in line for meat at the market."

* * *

Did you hear that Alitalia and El Al are merging to form a new airline?

It's going to be called Well I'll Tell Ya.

* * *

A Pole was so proud of his new red Cadillac that he just had to show it off; so he cruised through the black part of town. At a stop light a giant African-American hauled him out of the driver's seat, drew a circle around him in the road, and told him not to step out of the circle unless he wanted to get the shit beat out of him.

The hoodlum began to demolish the Caddie, starting with the headlights and windows when he heard the Pole laughing. He moved on to the body and engine, but in between crashes he couldn't help hearing the Pole's hysterical giggles. Finally the guy came over with his crowbar and said, "What in hell you laughin' at? Your fancy car's never gonna run again."

Snickering, the Pole replied, "So? Ever since you turned around I've been stepping in and out of this circle."

* * *

What do you get when you cross a Puerto Rican and a Chinese person?

A car thief who can't drive.

* * *

What's a Puerto Rican's idea of safe sex?

Locking the car door.

* * *

How can you tell if an Irishman's present at a cockfight?

He enters a duck.

How can you tell if a Pole is also there?

He bets on the duck.

And can you tell an Italian came, too?

The duck wins.

* * *

Did you hear about the juvenile delinquent from Beverly Hills?

He's too young to drive, so he only steals cars with chauffeurs in them.

* * *

What do you call an Indian butler?

Mahat Macoat.

* * *

Three men were hired to dig a six-foot ditch for the sanitation department. Soon the Italian laborer turned to his Polish buddy, who was slaving and sweating along next to him, and asked, "Say, how come we're down here doing all the work and he's up there telling us what to do?" He gestured at the third hired hand, an Irishman, who was standing atop the pile of dirt.

"Got me," said the Pole. "Why don't you go ask him?" So the Italian climbed out of the ditch and posed the question.

"Let me illustrate why I'm up here and you're down there," suggested the Irishman, placing his hand against a tree. "Hit my hand as hard as you can with your shovel."

The Italian happily obeyed, but the Irishman pulled his hand away at the last moment. With his hands aching and stinging from the force of the blow, the Italian was content to climb back down into the ditch.

"So how come we're down here and he's up there?" asked his buddy after a few minutes had passed in silence.

The Italian thought and thought, looking all around. Finally he held his hand up in front of his face and said, "Hit my hand as hard as you can with your shovel."

* * *

How do you clear out a K-Mart?

Yell, "Immigration!"

* * *

A Jew and a Chinese man were in a bar together. All of a sudden Grossman hauled off and slammed the Chinese guy so hard he fell right off his stool. "What the hell was that for?" asked poor Wang, staggering to his feet.

"That was for Pearl Harbor," was the explanation.

"The Japanese raided Pearl Harbor," Wang protested. "I'm Chinese, and I didn't have anything to do with it."

"Chinese, Japanese, they're all the same to me," said Grossman bluntly.

The conversation resumed, until the Chinese guy suddenly hauled off and knocked Grossman right on the floor.

"Hey, why'd you do that?" the Jew asked, crawling groggily back up onto his seat.

"That was for the *Titanic*," explained Wang.

"The *Titanic?!?* It was sunk by an iceberg," Grossman pointed out in an aggrieved tone.

"Iceberg, Goldberg, it's all the same to me."

* * *

What's the Irish version of foreplay?

"Brace yourself, Bridget!"

* * *

What do you call a fat Chinaman?

A Chunk.

* * *

A Pole and a Jew were in a bar watching TV when the late-night news came on. The lead story showed a berserk woman poised on a window ledge eleven stories up. "I'll bet you a hundred bucks she won't jump," said the Pole to the Jew.

"Deal," agreed the Jew, sticking out his hand a few minutes later when the woman plunged to a gory death. The Pole sadly forked over the money, only to look up in surprise as the other fellow tugged on his sleeve and offered him his money back. "You won it fair and square," he said, shaking his head.

"Not really," admitted the Jewish guy. "I saw it all happen on the six o'clock news."

"Me too," said the Pole, "but I never thought she'd do it again at eleven."

* * *

What do you get when you cross an Irishman and a Jew?

An alcoholic who buys his liquor wholesale.

* * *

13

What's the Haitian national anthem?

"Row, row, row your boat . . . "

* * *

Why do Mexicans drive low-riders?

So they can cruise and pick lettuce at the same time.

* * *

Italian woman: "Oh, Gino, you are the world's greatest lover!"

French woman: "Ah, Jacques, you are marvelous. More, more!"

Jewish woman: "Oy, Jake, the ceiling needs painting."

* * *

What do you say to a Puerto Rican in a three-piece suit?

"Will the defendant please rise?"

* * *

A Chinese man walked into a bar and said to the African-American bartender, "I'll have a jigger, nigger."

"You aren't trying to insult me, now were you, pal?" asked the bartender, his face tight with anger.

"Certainly not," the fellow assured him, shaking his head sincerely.

"So how about we change places?" he suggested, coming out from behind the bar. And when the customer had taken his place, the black man demanded, "Pour me a drink, chink."

"Sorry," replied the Chinese man firmly. "We don't serve niggers."

* * *

Why was the Irishman's second week in Alcoholics Anonymous so much easier than the first?

By the second week he was drinking again.

* * *

Did you hear the Army has developed an elite Special Forces Commando Group composed entirely of Hispanic soldiers?

In case of war, they're dropped behind enemy lines to strip the armored vehicles.

* * *

What's Jewish foreplay?

A trip to the jewelry store followed by half an hour of begging.

Puerto Rican foreplay?

"Is your husband back from work yet, Carmen?"

14

African-American foreplay?
"Don't scream or I'll kill you."

* * *

Did you hear about the new Japanese-Jewish restaurant?
It's called So-Sue-Mi.

* * *

A passerby watched the progress of two workmen from the Department of Parks as they moved down a Leningrad street. One stopped every twenty feet to dig a hole, the second filled it in as soon as he was done, then they moved on to the next site. Finally, overcome by curiosity, the observer asked what in heaven's name they were doing. "You certainly aren't accomplishing anything," she pointed out.

"You don't understand at all," protested the first worker indignantly. "We are usually a team of three: I dig the hole, Sergei plants the tree, and Vladimir packs the dirt back in. Today Sergei is home with the flu, but that doesn't mean Vladimir and I get to stop working, now does it?"

* * *

What food do you never see in Ethiopia?
After-dinner mints.

* * *

How do you know when an Ethiopian is pregnant?
You can see the baby.

* * *

How about the national anthem of Ethiopia?
"Aren't you hungry . . . ?"

* * *

What's invisible and smells like dirt?
Ethiopian farts.

* * *

What's so great about getting a blow job from an Ethiopian woman?
You know she'll drink every drop.

* * *

Why did the Ethiopian have a mouthful of dirt?
He was training to be a javelin.

* * *

It so happened that Myron Liebowitz and Vinnie D'Onofrio came of age at the same time. From his father, Vinnie received a brand new handgun, while at Myron's Bar Mitzvah on the other side of town, his father strapped a beautiful gold watch on his wrist. The next day after school Vinnie was full of admiration for the watch, while Myron was consumed with envy after one glance at the pistol. So the two friends decided to trade.

That night when Vinnie checked to see whether it was dinnertime, his father asked, "Where'd you get thatta watch?" And on hearing the story, he exploded. "Whatsa matter wid' yous? Here I am t'inkin' you gotta some brains in your head."

Vinnie looked frankly confused, so his father explained that some day Vinnie would probably fall in love and then he'd probably get married and then married life would probably get kind of dull. "An' somma day," he went on, "yous gonna find her in bed wit' anudda guy. An' whatta you gonna do then—look atta you watch and say, 'How long you gonna be?' "

* * *

What are the first three words a Puerto Rican child learns?

"Attention K-Mart shoppers . . . "

* * *

What are Bartles & James wine coolers called in Mexico?

Dos Okies.

* * *

Why do they let Puerto Ricans enlist in the armed forces?

So the African-American soldiers have someone to look down on.

* * *

A Jew, a Pole, and an African-American all died on the same day and were warmly greeted at the gates of Heaven by St. Peter. "Good to see you guys," said the saint. "One quick quiz, just a formality, and I'll be able to admit you."

"Hang on a sec," protested the Jew. "Being Jewish, I've had it rough all my life, and I'd like to know if there's any religious persecution in heaven."

"Certainly not," said St. Peter. "Spell *God*."

The Pole spoke up. "I've had to take so much shit all my life for being Polish, I'd like to make sure I'm not going to encounter any more of that sort of stuff in the afterlife."

"No way," St. Peter reassured him. "Spell *God*."

"St. Peter, I'm black, as you can see," said the African-

American, "and I've had to endure a lot of prejudice in my life. Can I expect any more of that here in Heaven?"

"Of course not," said St. Peter. "Spell *chrysanthemum*."

* * *

Seen the Canadian bumper sticker?

It says, "I'd Rather Be Driving."

* * *

How many Irishmen does it take to screw in a light bulb?

Two. One to hold the bulb, and the other to drink till the room spins.

* * *

And how many Teamsters does it take to change a light bulb?

Ten. You gotta PROBLEM with that?

* * *

What's the definition of a cad?

A Canadian who doesn't tell his wife he's sterile until after she's pregnant.

* * *

Who killed more Indians than Custer?

Union Carbide.

* * *

Two Poles couldn't figure out how to measure a flag pole they'd been hired to paint by the foot, so they asked a black guy who happened to be passing by if he would help.

The man pulled a pin out from the bottom of the flagpole, laid the pole on the ground, pulled out his ruler and measured it. When he was finished, he put his tape measure away, put the flag pole back in its stand, and left.

Once out of earshot, the one Polack turned to the other and said scornfully, "Now isn't that just like a black? You ask for the height and he gives you the width."

* * *

Why aren't there any Puerto Rican astronauts?

Because they'd honk the horn, squeal the tires, and play the radio too loud all the way to the moon.

* * *

Three addicts went into a favorite back alley to shoot up. The African-American addict sterilized his needle, swabbed it with alcohol, and shot up. Then he passed it to the Jewish junkie, who sterilized it, swabbed it with alcohol, and shot up. Then he passed

17

it to the Polish addict, who stuck the needle right in his arm.

"Are you crazy, man?" screamed the first two. "Haven't you heard of AIDS? You could get sick, man, you could *die*."

"Don't be ridiculous," said the Pole in a lofty tone. "*I'm* wearing a condom."

* * *

What do you get when you cross a black with a Japanese?

Someone who on December 7 has an uncontrollable urge to attack Pearl Bailey.

* * *

Miss DeAngelo was a none-too-bright Italian girl who had moved to Hollywood with dreams of becoming a star. She didn't find fame or glory, but she did encounter plenty of men willing to enjoy her plentiful charms, and eventually she found herself named in a divorce case.

When it was her turn on the stand, the prosecutor came forward. "Miss DeAngelo, the wife of the defendant has identified you as the 'other woman' in her husband's life. Now, do you admit that you went to the PriceRite Motel with this Mr. Evarts?"

"Well, yes," acknowledged Miss DeAngelo with a sniff, "but I couldn't help it."

"Couldn't help it?" sneered the lawyer. "How's that?"

"Mr. Evarts deceived me."

"Exactly what do you mean?"

"See, when we signed in," she explained, "he told the motel clerk I was his wife."

* * *

Heard about the black and the Mexican who opened up a restaurant?

It's called Nacho Mama.

* * *

Hear about the famous Polish doctor?

He performed the first successful hemorrhoid transplant.

* * *

The elderly Russian tottered down to the store to fetch his family's ration of meat, only to be informed that there was none to be had. Furious, the old man raged at the butcher for several minutes, cursing the wretched state of affairs in Russia, the endless lines, the inevitable shortages. And on his way out of the store he was approached by a sinister fellow in dark glasses and a black leather trenchcoat.

"Be careful, comrade," cautioned the man in a low voice. "If you had made a scene like this a few years ago, you know what would have happened to you." He pointed an imaginary pistol at the old fellow's temple, pulled the trigger, then walked off.

"What happened, Pyotr?" asked the old man's wife, seeing him return home empty-handed. "Did they run out of meat again?"

"It's worse than that," he replied glumly. "They've run out of bullets."

* * *

What's a wrench?

A place where people from New York raise cattle.

* * *

The young Irish bride made her first appointment with a gynecologist and told him of her and her husband's wish to start a family. "We've been trying for months now, Doctor Keith, and I don't seem to be able to get pregnant," she confessed miserably.

"I'm sure we'll solve the problem," the doctor reassured her. "If you'll just get up on the examining table and take off your underpants . . . "

"Well, all right, Doctor," agreed the young woman, blushing, "but I'd rather have my husband's baby."

* * *

Did you hear about the Italian who was asked to be a Jehovah's Witness?

He refused because he didn't see the accident.

* * *

What do you get when you cross a Jew and a gypsy?

A chain of empty stores.

* * *

A French couple, an Irish couple, and a Polish couple were having dinner together. The Frenchman says to his wife, "Pass me the sugar, sugar."

Not to be outdone, the Irishman asks his wife, "Could you pass me the honey, honey?"

Much impressed by these clever endearments, the Pole leans over to his wife and says, "Pass the pork, pig."

* * *

Why aren't there any swimming pools in Mexico?

Because all the Mexicans who can swim are already over here.

* * *

Why do Canadians like to do it doggie style?

So they can both keep watching the hockey game.

* * *

One day the Israeli soldier at the checkpoint addressed the Arab riding along the military highway on his donkey, his aged wife trudging before him. "I've been watching you go by every morning for months," the guard commented, "and you always ride and your wife is always on foot. Why?"

"Wife no have donkey," replied the Arab with a shrug.

"I see. But why does she walk in front of you? Is that the custom of your people?"

The Arab shook his head. "Land mines," he explained.

POLISH

A carload of Polish friends came across the scene of an accident. "Oh my God," gasped the driver, pulling over for a closer look at the crumpled sedan, "that looks like Joe's car." So they all piled out and walked closer.

"Look," said the second, "that's Joe's arm—I'd know that watch anywhere."

"I'm sure that's Joe's leg," said the third, pointing out where it lay against the curb.

"And look—that's definitely Joe's head," shouted the fourth, running after an object rolling slowly down the street. "Joe, Joe," he cried, picking it up. "Are you all right?"

* * *

Why did the Polish couple decide to have only four children?

Because they read that one out of every five babies born in the world is Chinese.

* * *

Kowalski started working weekends and late into the nights on a secret project. Finally, after months of work, he ran over to his friend Rositzke's house to show him the fruits of his labor. "Check this out," he said. "I made it." And he proudly handed his buddy a seventeen dollar bill.

"It's a beautiful counterfeit," said Rositzke admiringly, "but you're never going to get anywhere with a seventeen dollar bill."

"Oh, yeah?" Kowalski was furious. "Watch this." And he turned into the deli on the corner. A few minutes later he came out, beaming from ear to ear.

"Well?" asked Rositzke.

"Told you he'd give me change," declared Kowalski proudly. "And look: two seven dollar bills and a three."

* * *

Why was the Polish kid named Seven-and-Three-Eighths?
His mom picked his name out of a hat.

* * *

Exactly how stupid was the really stupid Pole?
He lit a match to see if he'd turned the lights out.

* * *

What's a Polish X-ray?
The doctor holds the patient up against a hundred-watt bulb.

* * *

Did you hear about the Polish inventor who worked for years on a cross between a toaster and an electric blanket?
He was going to sell it to people who wanted to pop out of bed.

* * *

He's also developing a new smoke detector—
It comes with a snooze alarm.

* * *

Kosinski backed through the door of the bar and came over to join his friend. His elbows were pressed against his ribs, his forearms stretched straight out in front of him, and his palms faced each other about eight inches apart. He sat down on a stool and ordered a beer, and when it came he turned to his friend. "Could you lift that glass to my mouth, please?"

His friend obliged, but couldn't help asking what was wrong. "Did you pull a muscle? Or have some kind of accident?"

"Oh, no," replied Kosinski. "Listen, I can't get to my wallet right now. Would you mind spotting me this round?"

His friend paid up, and fed Kosinski another swallow of beer. "So what's wrong with you? Some kind of weird disease?"

"Huh? Oh, I'm fine," Kosinski assured him.

"So what's the problem?" asked his friend, growing exasperated after a half hour of feeding Kosinski his beer.

"Problem? I don't have any problem," said Kosinski cheerfully. "My wife asked me to pick her up a pair of shoes on the way home, and this is her size."

* * *

Why wouldn't the Polish woman buy Easter seals?

She just knew feeding them would be a problem.

* * *

Did you hear about the new Polish supercalculator?

It's a giant hand with ten thousand fingers.

* * *

The Pole walked into the office and sidled up to his buddy. "Yo, Dubrowski," he said with a leer, "you gotta start pulling down the blind in your bedroom. Last night I got a real eyeful watching you and Lois go at it."

Dubrowski grinned broadly. "The joke's on you, Lenski," he responded. "I wasn't even home last night."

* * *

How come Polish construction workers only get half an hour for lunch?

The foreman doesn't want to have to retrain them.

* * *

Early one morning while his son was getting ready for his first day of school, a Polish father took him aside and proceeded to instruct him on the appropriate way to urinate: "Okay, son: one, unzip your pants; two, take out your penis; three, pull back the foreskin; four, pee into the urinal; five, shake your penis off; six, push back your foreskin; and finally, replace your penis and zip your fly back up."

Later that day, the father received a call from his son's teacher. "What seems to be the problem?" he asked.

"Well," the teacher said somewhat perplexed, "it appears that your son doesn't want to leave the bathroom."

"Oh, really? What's he doing in there?"

"We're not sure. He just keeps repeating, 'Three-six, Three-six.' "

* * *

How about the Polish kid whose teacher told him to write a hundred-word essay on what he did during summer vacation?

He wrote "Not much" fifty times.

* * *

What's this? (Puff out your cheeks.)

A Polish sperm bank.

* * *

An Irishman, an Italian, and a Pole were sitting at a bar. Ordering a drink, the Irishman said, "I hate this place. I know a place on State Street where I can get every third drink free."

"That's nothing," replied the Italian. "I know a joint over on the west side where every other drink is free."

"Oh yeah?" said the Pole. "Well I know a place on the south side where every drink is free and at the end of the night you can get laid in the parking lot!"

"No kidding?" asked his companions. "That sounds great—where'd you hear about it?"

"From my wife," the Pole said proudly.

* * *

Why did the Pole name his dog Herpes?

Because it wouldn't heel.

* * *

When the Pole walked into the corner bar late one night he was obviously steaming mad. He downed three shots before a friend came over and asked what was wrong.

"It's my wife, I can't believe it. When I got home tonight she was lying in bed all hot and bothered, and it made me suspicious. So I looked around, and sure enough, there was a naked guy hiding behind the shower curtain. Can you beat it?"

"Jesus. No wonder you're so pissed off," said his friend sympathetically.

"Yeah, but that's not all," the furious Pole went on. "That son of a bitch in the shower, he lied his way out of it."

* * *

The Polish father-to-be was pacing back and forth outside the hospital delivery-room door. Another nervous fellow finally broke the silence. "Some luck. My one week of vacation and look where I get to spend it."

"You think *you've* got bad luck?" responded the Pole. "I'm on my honeymoon."

* * *

Judge: "The charge is the theft of sixteen radios. Are you the defendant?"

Pole: "No sir. I'm the guy that stole the radios."

* * *

The basketball coach stormed into the university president's office and demanded a raise right then and there.

"Jesus Christ, man," protested President Kubritski, "you already make more than the entire English department."

"Yeah, maybe so, but you don't know what I have to put up with," the coach blustered. "Look." He went out into the hall and grabbed a jock who was jogging down the hallway. "Run over to my office and see if I'm there," he ordered.

Twenty minutes later the jock returned, sweaty and out of breath. "You're not there, sir," he reported.

"I see what you mean," conceded President Kubritski, scratching his head. "I would have phoned."

* * *

Then there was the Polish guy who ordered a pizza with everything on it. When it came out of the oven, they asked if he wanted it cut into four slices or eight.

"Make it four," decided the Pole. "I'll never be able to eat eight."

* * *

What does a Polish engineer say on his wedding night?

"Where's the reset button?"

* * *

The buxom Polish girl was stopped for speeding and hauled down to the police station. The desk sergeant looked her over, beckoned her into a back room, and unbuttoned his fly.

"Oh, no," cried the girl, "not another breathalyzer test!"

* * *

What was the Polish guy's idea of bondage?

Tying the woman's legs together.

* * *

Did you hear about the Polish dad who got horny one afternoon as the family was sitting around watching TV?

He said to his wife, "Let's send the kids to the S-H-O-W so we can fuck."

* * *

Why did the Polish hippie take two hits of LSD?

He wanted to go on a round trip.

* * *

A Polish couple and a single man are shipwrecked on a desert island. It doesn't take long for the single guy to get pretty horny, and finally he comes up with an idea for getting into the woman's pants. Climbing way up a tall palm tree, he hollers back down to the couple, "Hey y'all, quit fucking down there!" The Pole looks over at his wife—who's standing ten feet away—and says, "What the hell's he talking about?"

This goes on for several hours, until the married man is overcome with curiosity and decides to climb up the palm to see for himself what the other guy's problem is. As he's going up, the horny fellow jumps down to the beach, grabs the wife, and proceeds to screw her like crazy.

The Pole finally reaches the top of the palm tree, looks down, and says, "Goddamn if he wasn't right—it does look like they're fucking down there!"

* * *

What's the difference between a Polish girl and a bowling ball?

You can only fit three fingers in a bowling ball.

* * *

Walenski had joined the Army Airborne with dreams of parachuting, but now that the moment had come for his first jump, he was pretty scared. The instructor assured him that all he had to do was count to ten and pull the cord. "Relax—even if your chute malfunctions, the reserve will open automatically. And our truck will be waiting for you at the drop site." With those comforting words, the instructor gave Walenski a shove, and the young recruit found himself plummeting towards the earth.

After a few seconds of pure terror, the private began counting, and pulled the ripcord right on time. Nothing happened. Trying to stay calm, Walenski waited for the reserve chute to open. Nothing happened. "Shit," he muttered as the ground rushed towards him, "I'll just bet the truck isn't there either."

* * *

"Working hard, Stan?"

"Nah, I'm fooling the boss," replied the Pole with a wink. "He thinks I'm working, but I'm carrying the same load of cement up and down all day."

* * *

A Pole applied for a position as a night watchman at a lumberyard. "And do you feel you're qualified for such a responsible position?" the owner asked.

"Definitely, Mr. Reynolds," he replied promptly. "The slightest noise and I'm wide awake."

* * *

This guy came into work one day with a fistful of cigars and started passing them out left and right to celebrate the birth of his son. "Congratulations, Eric," said his boss. "How much did the baby weigh?"

"Four and a half pounds," reported the father proudly.

"Gee, that's kind of small."

"What did you expect?" retorted Eric indignantly. "We've only been married three months."

* * *

Did you hear about the adventurous Pole who got a zebra for a pet?

He named it Spot.

* * *

The manager of a prosperous whorehouse in Warsaw found to his dismay that he was running short of girls on a Saturday night. Thinking quickly, he dashed out and bought several inflatable sex dolls, figuring that, given his average clientele, no one would know the difference. Soon he ushered a customer into a room that housed one of the new lovelies, assuring him that he was in for an especially good time.

When the customer came out of the room a little while later, the manager was waiting eagerly in the hallway. He winked at the fellow and asked, "Well, how'd you like her?"

"I don't know what happened," the guy admitted, shaking his head. "I bit her on the tit, she farted, and flew out the window."

* * *

Know why they don't use the 911 system in Poland?

Because the Poles can't find "11" on their telephones.

* * *

Did you hear the two biggest lies in Poland?

1) The check is in your mouth; and

2) I won't come in the mail.

* * *

A Pole is walking down the street and passes a hardware store advertising a sale on a chainsaw capable of cutting seven hundred trees in seven hours. Figuring that's a hell of a deal, the Pole decides to buy one.

The next day, he comes back with the saw and complains to the salesman that the thing didn't come close to chopping down the seven hundred trees the ad promised.

"Well," suggests the salesman, "let's test it out back."

Finding a log, the salesman pulls the starter cord and the saw makes a great roaring sound.

The Pole jumps back in alarm. "What the hell was that?"

* * *

How come nobody in Poland drinks Kool-Aid?

They can't figure out how to get a quart of water into that little envelope.

* * *

Zabiski saved up his money for an excursion to Reno, where he soon found himself at the bar next to a very attractive brunette. "Say, could I buy you a drink?" he asked boldly.

"Forget it buddy," she replied, not unkindly. "I'm gay."

Zabiski looked blank.

"I'm a lesbian," she elaborated.

Zabiski shook his head. "What's a lesbian?"

"See that woman over there?" She pointed at a lovely blond waitress serving drinks on the far side of the room.

Zabiski nodded, perking up.

"Well, I'd like to take her up to my room," the brunette explained, "take all her clothes off, and nibble her tits and lick every curve and suck every inch of that sweet young thing, all night long."

At this, Zabiski burst into tears and buried his head in his arms. "Why the hell're you crying?" asked his companion gruffly.

"I think I'm a lesbian too," he sobbed.

* * *

How can you spot the Polish secretary?

She's the one with white-out all over her computer screen.

* * *

"Now with that entrée, either a white wine or a light red would be appropriate," the waiter graciously pointed out. "What may I serve you?"

"Suit yourself," replied the Polish diner cheerfully. "I'm colorblind."

* * *

How did the Germans capture Poland so easily?

They marched in backwards and said they were leaving.

* * *

"Daddy, here's a note from the teacher," said the little boy when he got home from school. "I'll read it to you: 'Dear Mr. Rubiak: Stash really ought to have the use of an encyclopedia.' Well, Dad, what about it?"

Without lifting his head from the racing form, Rubiak grunted, "I walked to school when I was a kid, and so can you."

* * *

A Pole was working at a construction site where the boss left each day at 11:00 A.M. and was gone for two hours. This became such a regular occurrence that the rest of the workers decided to spend the two hours in the bar across the street, but the Pole decided to head home for some extra nookie. When he arrived home, he found his boss busy banging his wife in the bedroom! Well, he walked right out and headed back to the job.

The following day the Pole was working his ass off when everyone headed across to the bar. "Hey, Ski, aren't you coming?" asked one of them.

"Hell no," said the Pole. "Yesterday I almost got caught!"

* * *

What does a Polish girl get on her wedding night that's long and hard?

A new last name.

* * *

A stranger walks into a bar and announces to the barman, "Hey, fellas! Have I got some hilarious Polish jokes for you guys."

The bartender leans over to him and says, "Listen, if I were you I'd watch your tongue. Those two-hundred-and-fifty pound bouncers are both Polish, I ain't no midget and I'm Polish, and so's every other guy in here."

"Oh, that's okay," says the stranger cheerfully. "I'll talk v-e-r-y s-l-o-w-l-y."

* * *

How come there are no Polish pharmacists?

They can't fit the little bottles in the typewriters.

* * *

A Polish guy met a woman in a bar and she accepted his invitation to come back to his place. After a few drinks and some soft music, the Pole suggested retiring to the bedroom; and she was quite willing. One thing led to another, and soon they were going at it hot and heavy.

But right in the middle of everything the Pole stopped dead, looked at her and asked, "Hey, you don't have herpes, do you?"

"No way!" she replied.

"That's a relief," he admitted. "The last girl didn't tell me until it was too late."

* * *

Did you hear about the Pole who was so thick the other Poles noticed?

* * *

Jerzy and Latvia were bored one day and decided to go to the zoo and taunt the gorillas. As they made faces at the apes, they didn't notice that one of the animals was getting quite turned on by Latvia's tits. All of a sudden, the ape reached through the bars, grabbed hold of Latvia's blouse, and pulled her into his cage.

"What should I do!?" she screamed at Jerzy as the gorilla tore her shirt off and started to sexually assault her.

"I dunno." Jerzy looked blank. "Tell him what you tell me all the time: that you have a headache."

* * *

Two Polish guys went off on their annual hunting expedition, and by accident one got shot. His worried companion got him out of the deep woods, into the car, and rushed him to the nearest hospital. "Well, Doc," he asked anxiously in the emergency room, "is he going to make it?"

"Tough call," admitted the physician. "He'd have a better chance if you hadn't gutted him first."

* * *

Why don't Poles go elephant hunting?

They can't lift the decoys.

* * *

A Pole makes an appointment with his doctor because his hemorrhoids are really bothering him. The doctor gives him some suppositories and tells him to come back in a week for a checkup. "How's it going?" he asks.

"I gotta tell you, Doc," replies the Pole, "for all the good those pills did me, I coulda shoved them up my ass."

* * *

How does a Pole rob a drive-in window at the bank?

He puts his gun in the little basket along with a note that says, "This is a stick-up."

* * *

Did you hear about the first Polish astronaut to walk in space?

When he knocked on the door of the space capsule to be let back in, the other astronaut said, "Who's there?"

* * *

When her parents asked what she wanted for her birthday, the punctual little Polish girl said, "I wanna watch."

So they let her.

* * *

The pilot and copilot of a transcontinental flight are chatting in the cockpit when the copilot notices one of the four jet engines catching fire. "Gee, Bob, how're we going to cope with this?" he asks a bit nervously.

"No problem. Listen." The pilot picks up the microphone and announces, "Attention, passengers: This flight will be twenty minutes late." Replacing the microphone, he winks knowingly at the copilot.

Ten minutes later, engine two quits. "Attention, passengers. We will be forty minutes late arriving at our destination."

Pretty soon engine number three conks out. This time the pilot announces, "Attention, passengers. We will be an hour and a half late."

Two Poles in economy class look at each other and one remarks, "Gosh, if that fourth engines goes, we'll be up here all night."

* * *

Did you hear about the Polish gynecologist who used two fingers?

He wanted a second opinion.

* * *

Why did the Polish man laugh as his house was burning down?

He knew he had enough wood in the attic to build another one.

* * *

A young Polish girl was hitchhiking along the interstate and a big semi pulled over to pick her up. The driver was a serious CB addict, and the dashboard boasted an enormous CB radio.

"That's the best radio ever made," he told the bug-eyed girl. "You can talk anywhere in the world on it."

"No kidding," she gasped. "Boy, I would really love to talk to my mother in Poland."

"Oh, yeah?"

"I'd give anything to talk to my mother in Poland."

"Anything?" he pressed.

"*Anything*," she assured him.

"Maybe we can work something out," he suggested with a lewd wink. And he pulled his erect penis out of his pants.

The girl leaned over, took a deep breath, and yelled, "HELLO, MOM?"

* * *

Did you hear about the Polish man who had a penis transplant?

His hand rejected it.

* * *

How about the Polish seaman who wanted to be buried at sea?

Both his sons drowned digging his grave.

* * *

A Polish guy came home from work early to find his wife lying on the bed, sweaty and out of breath. "Honey, I think I'm having a heart attack," she gasped. The Pole ran downstairs to call the doctor, and on the way his little son tugged at his sleeve and said, "Daddy, Daddy, there's a naked man in the closet."

The Pole ran back upstairs, opened the closet, pulled out his best friend, and yelled, "Jesus, Larry, Marie's having a heart attack and here you are, scaring the kids!"

* * *

How come the Pole returned his necktie?

It was too tight.

* * *

Why do Polish names end in "ski?"

They don't know how to spell "toboggan."

* * *

Can you figure out why Poland's going to declare war on us in about fifteen years?

That's when they're going to start understanding these jokes.

AFRICAN-AMERICAN

What did George Washington and Thomas Jefferson have in common?

They were the last white people to have these names.

* * *

This African-American walked into a bar with a beautiful parrot perched on his shoulder. "Say, that's really something," commented the bartender admiringly. "Where'd you get it?"

"Africa," replied the parrot.

* * *

What do you call a black hitchhiker?

Stranded.

* * *

Heard about the new toy store in Harlem?

It's called "We Be Toys."

* * *

An elderly Southern planter checked into the hospital in pretty bad shape, and was soon informed by the doctor that he needed a heart transplant. "All right, Doctor Greenstein," said the planter, signing the insurance papers. "But I have one request: Could you please give me a white man's heart?" The cardiologist promised to do what he could.

When the Southerner woke up after the operation, the doctor told him he had some bad news and some good news. "I'm afraid I had to use a black man's heart," he gravely informed his patient. The patient paled. "But here's the bright side: Your dick's three inches longer."

* * *

Did you hear about the rural Alabama high school's production of Snow White and the Seven Dwarfs?

They had to bus in Snow White.

* * *

What do you call a black Frenchman?

Jacques Custodian.

* * *

How do you keep little black kids from jumping up and down on the bed?

Put Velcro on the ceiling.

* * *

What do you call Mike Tyson with no arms and no legs?

"Yo, nigger!"

* * *

Did you hear about the new French restaurant under African-American ownership?

It's called Chez What.

* * *

How do you make a black person nervous?

Take him to an auction.

* * *

The top brass at NASA was getting flak about never having sent an African-American astronaut to the moon, so the next moon shot went up with a black astronaut aboard. The only hitch was that the decision had been so sudden that the fellow hadn't even been briefed. His only instructions were to strap himself in, wait till he reached an altitude of five miles, and remove his helmet. The craft was on complete automatic pilot, so Mission Control wasn't too worried.

On the way up the astronaut had plenty of time to reflect on how the hell he was going to occupy himself during the flight, and to wish he had some real responsibility. As he was musing, the spacecraft reached the designated altitude, and as the astronaut removed his helmet he was startled to hear a noise from elsewhere on the ship. Investigating, he was shocked to come across another passenger, a chimpanzee in full astronaut garb! The monkey, too, had just removed his helmet, but it seemed to be studying a computer terminal in front of its seat.

"I don't have a terminal," the astronaut thought to himself. "What's going on here?" Looking over the chimp's shoulders, he saw that the screen contained a list of operating instructions for the mission's data-gathering operations. His worst fears were confirmed when, in shock, he read the last item on the list:

1800 HOURS—FEED THE ASTRONAUT.

* * *

How about the Japanese factory that spray-painted all their new robots black?

They were two hours late to work the next day.

* * *

Why are there so few African-American skiers?

Because it's not easy to ski with a pole in one hand and a boom box in the other.

* * *

Leroy was plenty nervous when he was served with a subpoena in a paternity suit. "I gotta go to the clinic and get a blood test to see if those twins of Tanya's are mine," he moaned to his best friend Tyrone.

He was a nervous wreck the morning of the test. "Last thing I need is two more babies to pay for, and Tiantha'll have my ass," he complained. But when he came out of the clinic, Leroy was calm and happy.

"So, they find out if you're the daddy or not?" asked Tyrone eagerly.

"Shit no," answered Leroy with a grin. "That nurse was so dumb, she took the blood out of my finger!"

* * *

What has six legs and goes, "Ho-de-do, ho-de-do, ho-de-do?"

Three African-Americans running for the elevator.

* * *

It was the first day of the fall term at Princeton, and an African-American freshman was learning his way around the campus. Stopping a distinguished-looking upperclassman, he inquired, "Say, can you tell me where the library is at?"

"My good fellow," the upperclassman replied haughtily, "at Princeton we do not end our sentences with a preposition."

"All right," said the freshman, "can you tell me where the library is at, asshole?"

* * *

What's the difference between a black and a bicycle?

A bicycle doesn't sing, "Kumbaya, my lord" when you chain it to the wall.

* * *

Miss Struthers asked her fifth graders to name the most important invention in the history of the world. "Yes, Luanne," she began, pointing at a little girl in the front row.

"The plane, Miss Struthers," she replied. "Now people can travel really far, really easily and fast."

"Yes, Billy?" The teacher nodded at a little boy who suggested the telephone. "It makes it so people from all over the world can talk to each other."

"Very good, Billy."

"Miss Struthers, I know, I know!" The teacher turned, surprised, to a little black kid in the back row who was waving his arm and jumping up and down in his seat.

"Yes, Marcus? Go ahead."

"It's the thermos, Miss Struthers. It keeps hot things hot and cold things cold—and *how* do it *know*?"

* * *

What did the police artist sketch when the woman described her rapist as blond, blue-eyed, and 5'6"?

A big, bad-looking black kid.

And what did she say when she looked at the sketch?

"That's him."

* * *

What was the name of the black Secretary of the Interior?

James Say Watt.

* * *

Why did God give African-Americans such big dicks?

Because He was so sorry about what He'd done to their hair.

* * *

Why do schoolchildren prefer white teachers to African-American teachers?

Because white teachers are easier to see in front of the blackboard.

* * *

A storefront opened up in Harlem offering a radical "decolorization" process which promised to lighten even the darkest skin and eyes—for the budget price of ninety-nine dollars.

Otis and Manfred saved up their money, and with cash in hand, Otis dragged his friend over to the shop with him. In he went, emerging in half an hour with white skin and blond hair. Manfred's eyes bulged. "Hey, man, you look *fine*. Listen, I only got ninety-eight dollars—can you spare me the extra dollar?"

Otis's blue eyes narrowed as he snapped, "Go get a job."

* * *

Heard about the new breakfast cereal aimed at African-American men?

It's called, "Nuthin', Bitch."

* * *

Why was there only one African-American astronaut aboard the *Challenger*?

They didn't know it was going to explode.

* * *

The poor black boy from Macon, Georgia, felt a wave of panic come over him as he surveyed the all-white jury in the New Hampshire courthouse. Positive he'd never beat the murder rap, he managed to get hold of one of the kindlier-looking jurors, and bribe her with his life savings to go for a manslaughter verdict.

Sure enough, at the close of the trial the jury declared him guilty of manslaughter. Tears of gratitude welling up in his eyes, the young man had a moment with the juror before being led off to prison. "Thank you, thank you—how'd you do it?"

"It wasn't easy," she admitted. "They all wanted to acquit you."

* * *

Did you hear about the ad for BMWs in *Ebony*?

It says, "You've got the radio—now get the car."

* * *

What do steroids and the South African government have in common?

They both make blacks run faster.

* * *

Hear about the new synagogue in Harlem?

It's called Temple Beth-You-Is-My-Woman-Now.

JEWISH

An extremely pale, slight man wearing dark glasses stood out from the usual crowd at a Miami Beach pool. Mrs. Kravitz took an immediate interest in the newcomer. Settling herself next to his deck chair, she introduced herself and asked, "Why so pale?"

"Leave me alone, lady," grunted the man, "I just got outta jail."

"Oh, I see," said Mrs. Kravitz, pursing her lips. "How long for?"

"Five years."

"That's terrible," she clucked. "For what?"

"Embezzlement."

"Ooh." Mrs. Kravitz nodded knowledgeably.

"And then five years for armed robbery," said the man in a sudden burst of talkativeness, "and then another lousy ten."

"And what was that for?"

"I killed my wife."

A big smile coming over her face, Mrs. Kravitz sat bolt upright. "Myrna," she shouted to her friend across the pool, "he's *single!*"

* * *

What's a JAP's idea of natural childbirth?

Absolutely no makeup.

* * *

How many Jews does it take to screw in a light bulb?

Three. One to call the cleaning lady, and the other two to feel guilty about having to call the cleaning lady.

* * *

Did you hear that a Jewish consortium's taken over Irving Trust? They're renaming it Trust Irving.

* * *

All Jewish mothers carry a card in their wallets. What does it say?
"In case of an accident, I'm not surprised."

* * *

How can you tell it's a Jewish mother's home?
There's a safety mat in the bird bath.

* * *

At the conclusion of the physical exam the doctor summoned his patient into his office with a very grave look on his face. "I hate to be the one to break it to you, Fred," he said, "but you've only got six months to live."

"Oh my God," gasped Fred, turning white. When the news had sunk in he said, "Listen, Doc, you've known me a long time. Do you have any suggestions as to how I could make the most of my remaining months?"

"Have you ever married?" asked the doctor.

Fred shook his head.

"You might think about it. After all you'll need someone to look after you during the final illness."

"Good point, Doc," mused Fred.

"One more suggestion," continued the doctor. "Marry a Jewish girl."

"A Jewish girl—how come?" wondered Fred.

"It'll seem longer."

* * *

What happens when a Jew with an erection walks into a wall?
He breaks his nose.

* * *

Halfway through World War II Adolph Hitler consulted a clairvoyant to find out on what day he would die. He almost fell off the little gilt chair when she informed him that his death would fall on a Jewish holiday.

"Me—impossible!" protested the corporal. "Which Jewish holiday?"

"Mein Führer," the fortune teller pointed out knowingly, "any day you die will be a Jewish holiday."

* * *

What did the little old Jewish lady say to the flasher when he threw open his raincoat and exposed himself?

"You call *that* a lining?"

* * *

The phone rang in the obituary department of the Miami newspaper. "How much does it cost to have an obituary printed?" asked an elderly woman.

"It's five dollars a word, ma'am," replied the clerk politely.

"Fine," said the old woman after a brief pause. "Got a pencil?"

"Yes, ma'am."

"Got some paper?"

"Yes, ma'am."

"Okay, write this down: 'Cohen dead.' "

"That's it?" asked the clerk disbelievingly.

"That's it."

"I'm sorry, I should have told you, ma'am—there's a five-word minimum."

"Yes you should've, young man," complained the old woman. "Now let me think a minute. . . . All right, got a pencil?"

"Yes, ma'am."

"Got some paper?"

"Yes, ma'am."

"Okay, here goes: 'Cohen dead. Cadillac for Sale.' "

* * *

What do you get when you cross Arnold Schwarzenegger with a Hasidic Jew?

Conan the Distributor.

* * *

What's the difference between a Libyan terrorist and a JAP?

A terrorist makes fewer demands.

* * *

You can imagine the excitement when a Martian spaceship landed in a sunny suburban field and proved to be filled with intelligent, amicable beings. The very next morning the head Martian appeared on a national television talk show. "Tell me," asked the interviewer, clearing her throat nervously, "do all of your people have seven fingers and toes?"

"Yes, we do," replied the Martian, gracefully waving his slender green appendages in the air.

"And two heads? Everyone is born with those?"

"Oh, yes," answered the Martian, nodding both enthusiastically.

"And also those lovely diamonds and rubies embedded in their chest scales?"

"Certainly not," snapped the Martian. "Only the Jews."

* * *

Why does a Jewish bride smile on her wedding night?

Because she's given her last blow job.

* * *

Did you hear about the JAP who asked her father for fifty dollars to go shopping?

"Forty dollars," he screamed, "what're you gonna buy with thirty dollars?"

* * *

What do you call a Japanese JAP?

An Orienta.

* * *

One Sunday, an old Jewish man walked into a Catholic church and sits down in a confessional.

"Forgive me, Father, for I have sinned," he said humbly. "Yesterday afternoon a beautiful girl with gigantic breasts and a cute little tush valked into my delicatessen and started making nice to me. Vell, what can I tell you, I closed the store and for the next six hours I fucked her. I vas like a crazy man or something."

"Excuse me, Mr. Epstein," interrupted a perplexed priest, "but you're Jewish. Why are you telling me?"

"Telling *you*?" exulted Epstein. "I'm telling everyone!"

* * *

Did you hear about the Jewish porn movie?

It's called, "Debbie Does Bubkis."

* * *

What does a Southern Jew say?

"*Chai*, y'all!"

* * *

Why does a Jewish divorce cost so much?

It's worth it.

* * *

When do Jewish men stop masturbating?
When their wives die.

* * *

Three respectable Jewish widows decided to go on a photographic safari to East Africa. The expedition pitched its tents deep in the jungle and the next morning set out on its first excursion, but Naomi was too tired to go along. To her companions' dismay, she stayed alone at the campsite, and no sooner were they out of ear-shot than a huge gorilla swung down from a tree, grabbed the woman, and dragged her off to his nest to screw her mercilessly for three days. The following morning Sophie and Zelda, nearly out of their minds with worry and grief, found a battered and bloody Naomi outside their tent. She was airlifted back to Mt. Sinai hospital in New York, where her two friends hovered by the bedside as she drifted in and out of consciousness. Finally she appeared to come to her senses, and a huge tear crept down her cheek.

"Naomi, darling, speak to us," beseeched her friends. "Did that creature abuse you? Are you in pain? Why are you crying?"

"What's to say?" sobbed Naomi. "He never calls, he never writes. . . . "

* * *

What's the definition of a Jewish dilemma?
Free ham.

* * *

When Ira came into the temple, he spotted his friend Ezra sitting in the back row looking forlorn. "Why the long face?" he whispered, sitting down next to his friend.

"Two months ago my uncle Milton died, left me thirty thousand dollars."

"I'm sorry to hear of your loss. Were you and he very close?" asked Ira solicitously.

"That's not all," said Ezra. "Just last month my great-aunt Sadie passed away. She left me fifty thousand dollars."

"Two loved ones lost in two months . . . no wonder you're depressed."

"Oh, that's not what's wrong," Ezra went on mournfully.

"No? Then what?" asked his friend.

"This month, nothing!"

* * *

Did you hear about the bum who walked up to the Jewish mother and said, "Lady, I haven't eaten in three days"?

She said, "Force yourself."

* * *

What's the difference between a JAP and poverty?

Poverty sucks.

* * *

Three Jewish mothers were sitting around comparing notes on their exemplary offspring. "There never was a daughter more devoted than my Judy," said Mrs. Levine with a sniff. "Every summer she takes me to the Catskills for a week, and every winter we spend a week in Delray Beach."

"That's nothing compared to what my Lois does for me," declared Mrs. Klein proudly. "Every winter she treats me to two weeks in Miami, and in the summer two weeks in the Hamptons, in my private guest house."

Mrs. Lipkin sat back with a proud smile. "Nobody loves her mother like my Patty does, nobody."

"So what does she do?" asked the two women, turning to her.

"Three times a week she gets into a cab, goes to the best psychiatrist in the city, and pays him one hundred and fifty dollars an hour—*just to talk about me!*"

* * *

How many JAPs does it take to change a light bulb?

Two. One to call Daddy and one to get the Diet Pepsi.

* * *

How many Jewish mothers does it take to change a light bulb?

None. "Don't worry about me, I'll sit in the dark . . . "

* * *

The elderly Jewish woman was terribly proud of her two-year-old grandson, and took him down with her to Miami. The first morning she got him all decked out and set him down on the sand to play. But no sooner had she settled herself in her beach chair than a huge wave came up and swept the baby away.

"God," she cried, standing up and shaking her fist at the sky, "you've got some nerve! How dare you take away this darling boy, who's barely had a chance to live? Think of his poor parents, not to mention what it'll do to me, a devoted Jew! That baby deserves a long and happy life—bring him back to his loved ones. Bring him *back!*"

In another instant the wave returned, setting the toddler down unharmed on the sand. The grandmother looked him over, looked right back up at the sky, and snapped, "He had a hat!"

* * *

What's the worst thing for a JAP about having a colostomy?

Trying to find shoes to match the bag.

* * *

How does a JAP eat a banana? (This is a visual joke, so pay attention.)

Pretend you are holding a banana with your right hand. With the other hand, peel the banana halfway down. Continuing to hold the banana in your right hand, put your left hand behind your head, open your mouth, and push your head down over the banana.

* * *

Two Jewish women are comparing maladies. "Oy, have I got a sore throat," complains Selma.

"When I have a sore throat I suck on a Lifesaver," says Sadie.

Selma sniffs. "Easy for you, you live at the beach."

* * *

What do you get when you cross a JAP and an Apple?

A computer that never goes down.

* * *

Did you hear about the new Jewish bank?

When you call up, the teller complains, "You never visit. You never write. You only call when you want money."

* * *

A young Jewish man takes his mother to a movie about life in ancient Rome. She's from the old country and has a little difficulty following the customs in this strange land, so at one point she asks her son to explain a scene in progress. "This particular scene," he whispers, "shows how in those days the Romans often persecuted the Christians by throwing them in the arena to be devoured by lions."

Studying the gory image for a few moments, she points her finger at a lion in the far corner and asks, "And dat vun—vy isn't he eating?"

* * *

What's the difference between a Jew and an elephant?

Elephants eventually forget.

* * *

A devout Jew, Mrs. Feinstein offered up her prayers each week in temple. One week she prayed especially fervently. "Lord, I have always been good, and I've led a fine life. I only have one complaint: I'm poor. Please, Lord, let me win the lottery."

The next week, Mrs. Feinstein was a little more strident. "Lord," she prayed, "have I ever missed a High Holy Day? Not fasted on Yom Kippur? Why must I go to my grave a pauper? One lottery win is all I'm asking You for."

The third week Mrs. Feinstein made no bones about her displeasure. "A faithful Jew such as myself, Lord, always observant, always dutiful, asks for one little favor, and what do I get . . . ?"

A glowing, white-bearded figure stepped down from the heavens into the temple. "Now, Mrs. Feinstein," boomed God, "don't you think you could at least meet me half way, and buy a ticket?"

* * *

Did you hear about the Jewish robber?

He walks into stores with a pricing gun and says, "Hand over your cash or I'll mark down every item in here."

* * *

Milton came into his wife's dressing room one day after work and perched nervously on the edge of her chaise longue. "Debby, if I were, say, disfigured, would you still love me," he asked.

"Darling, I'll always love you," she said calmly, filing her nails.

"How about if I became impotent, couldn't make love to you any more?" he asked anxiously.

"Don't worry, darling, I'll always love you," she told him, buffing her nails.

"Well, how about if I lost my job as vice president?" Milton went on. "What if I weren't pulling in six figures anymore? Would you still love me then?"

The JAP looked over at her husband's worried face. "Milton, I'll always love you," she assured him, "but most of all, I'll really miss you."

* * *

Why do Jewish girls think prostitution is such a good business?

"Ya got it, ya sell it, ya still got it!"

* * *

An old Jew was retiring from the string and twine business. "Herschel," he implored his best friend, "I got one last load of string. Buy me out so I can retire with an empty shop and a clear heart."

Herschel had no interest in purchasing a load of string but his old friend's impassioned pleading finally wore him down. "Myron, all right, all right," he finally conceded. "I'll buy some of your string—enough to reach from the tip of your nose to the tip of your dick."

To Herschel's surprise, his friend embraced him warmly and left without another word. He was even more surprised when a truck arrived the next morning loaded with a massive roll of string. "Myron, what is this!" he screamed at his friend over the phone.

"My nose is in Palm Beach," explained Myron happily, "but the tip of my dick is buried somewhere outside Minsk."

* * *

Did you hear about the new movie called *Altered Suits*?

It's the story of a Jewish man who takes acid and buys retail.

* * *

Mr. Cohen emigrated to the United States as a young man and fulfilled the immigrant's dream: He ran his own profitable nail factory in Brooklyn, bought a nice house, sent his kids to college, even put the oldest son through Harvard Business School. When the young man graduated, Mr. Cohen said to him, "Harvey, you're a smart boy—I'm turning the business over to you and retiring to Florida."

A year later he got an excited phone call from Harvey. "Dad, things are going great: I've got computerized inventory, an automated production line, even a great new ad campaign. You've gotta come see it with your own eyes."

So he picked his father up at the airport, and just before they reached the factory a huge billboard loomed up. It was a close-up of Jesus on the cross, with the slogan USE COHEN'S NAILS FOR THE TOUGHEST JOBS. "Oy, Harvey," groaned Cohen, "*that's* your new campaign? I'm telling you, the goys are never gonna go for it."

A year later Harvey called his father again. "Dad, you've gotta come up again and see how great things are going! And by the way, you were right about that ad campaign. We've got a whole new one running now."

So Cohen got on a plane to New York, and on the way in from the airport he saw the same huge billboard. Only this time the picture was of Jesus crumpled at the foot of the cross, and the slogan read YOU SHOULDA USED COHEN'S NAILS.

* * *

How can you spot a disadvantaged Jewish teenager?

He's driving a domestic car.

* * *

When Selma answered her phone, it happened to be an obscene call. The man on the other end began describing in detail all the kinky, perverted sexual acts he wanted to engage in with her.

"Now hang on, wait just a minute," Selma interrupted. "All this you know from the way I said hello?"

WASP

What's a WASP's idea of open-mindedness?
    Dating a Canadian.

* * *

What positions do WASPs screw in?
    "Positions?!?"

* * *

How can you tell a WASP kid?
    He's the one who asks for his allowance in Deutschmarks.

* * *

How can you spot an inflatable sex doll designed especially for WASPs?
    It has no hole.

* * *

The WASP couple met at the squash club. After a Perrier and a comparison of their respective professional accomplishments, the girl said, "Well, your place or mine?"
    The guy shrugged. "Hey, if it's going to be a hassle, forget it."

* * *

How can you tell if a WASP is a really fabulous lover?
    When his wife loses her place in her book more than once.

* * *

How can you spot a WASP household?
    The *TV Guide*'s in hardcover.

* * *

Why do WASPs fly so much?
    For the food.

* * *

Did you hear about the WASP mother who finally pinpointed the cause of teenage pregnancy?

It's called a "date."

* * *

Mopsy sulked right through the cocktail hour and well into dinner, and finally her husband couldn't take it any more. "What's wrong, darling?" he asked.

"That horrid Betsy Bridgeport ordered the very same dress from Saks that I was planning to wear to Bunny's wedding," she replied with a pout.

"And I suppose you'd like to buy a new one?" he asked wearily.

"Well," Mopsy pointed out, after reflecting briefly, "it would be a lot cheaper than moving."

* * *

How many WASPs does it take to change a light bulb?

One.

* * *

What's WASP foreplay?

An engagement ring.

* * *

How can you tell the bride at a WASP wedding?

She's the one kissing the golden retriever.

* * *

What do WASPs do instead of making love?

Rule the country.

* * *

Why did God create WASPs?

Somebody had to buy retail.

* * *

How many WASPs does it take to plan a trip to Israel?

Two, one to ask where and one to ask why.

* * *

What's a WASP's idea of mass transit?

The ferry to Martha's Vineyard.

* * *

Hear about the disadvantaged WASP?

He grew up with a black-and-white TV.

* * *

After a very sheltered childhood, it was mildly surprising that Hackley managed to get a decent job, to persuade a nice girl to marry him, and to father a son and heir. "Now darling," coached his wife, "don't forget to drop by St. Thomas's and ask the Rector to arrange for Hackley Junior's christening."

"Are you sure about that?" the proud father asked, peering dimly down at the tiny squalling bundle. "He seems awfully small to have a bottle smashed over his head."

* * *

What do you get when you cross a WASP and a Mexican?

A migrant stockbroker.

* * *

What do you get when you cross a WASP and an African-American?

An abortion.

* * *

"We have a new baby at our house," reported Spencer to Chandler at tumbling class.

"Neat! Is it a boy or a girl?"

"I don't know," admitted Spencer. "They haven't dressed it yet."

* * *

Young Mrs. Townsend wanted very much to participate in the correct charities, and when the annual Junior League Easter Charity Ball came around, she volunteered to head the committee. It took a lot of organizing, but the party went off without a hitch, and she dined and danced into the wee hours.

When the festivities finally drew to a close, she was dismayed to observe a bag lady bundled on the sidewalk next to her Saab Turbo. Hearing the rustle of Mrs. Townsend's taffeta skirts, the old woman extended a grimy palm and asked the socialite if she could spare any change.

"Oooh, the nerve," gasped Mrs. Townsend, "and after I spend all night slaving away! Aren't people like you *ever* satisfied?"

* * *

Definition of a WASP:

Someone who thinks Taco Bell is the Mexican phone company.

* * *

51

How can you tell the Episcopal priest at the ecumenical ceremony?
He's the one who sends back the wine.

* * *

Why do WASPs play golf?
It's the only chance they get to dress up like black people.

HANDICAPPED

What do you call a hippy with no legs?
A veteran.

* * *

Why don't midgets use Tampax?
They'd trip on the strings.

* * *

Three extremely pregnant women were knitting away to pass the time in the obstetrician's waiting room. After a little while one woman put down her knitting and took a pill.

"If you don't mind me asking, what kind of pill are you taking?" asked one of the other expectant mothers.

"Iron," she replied. "I don't want my baby to be anemic."

Soon a second woman also stopped to swallow a pill. "Calcium," she replied in answer to the same question. "I want my baby to have strong bones."

And a while later the third woman put down her knitting and popped a pill. "Thalidomide," she explained matter-of-factly. "I don't know how to knit sleeves."

* * *

How can you tell a pervert is really a loser?
When blowing up his inflatable doll gives him a headache.

* * *

What does a one-legged ballerina wear?
A one-one.

* * *

Mrs. Jones began to get nervous when dark fell and her husband hadn't returned from his regular Saturday golf game. Dinnertime came and went and she became more and more anxious, so when she heard his car pull in, she rushed out to the driveway. "Where've you been? I've been worried sick!" she exclaimed.

"Harry had a heart attack on the third hole," her husband explained.

"Oh, no! That's terrible."

"You're telling me," moaned her husband. "All day long it was hit the ball, drag Harry, hit the ball, drag Harry . . . "

* * *

Susie was scheduled for surgery on her mouth, and the night before the operation she was a nervous wreck. Finally, she confessed her darkest fears to the night nurse. "What if Dr. Levine's hand slips?" she asked. "What if I'm horribly disfigured for the rest of my life?"

"You really don't need to worry," said the nurse soothingly. "Dr. Levine is a superb surgeon. Why, people who need oral surgery fly in from all over the world to consult with him."

Susie sighed with relief. "You're right, of course. Why, once I come out of anesthesia, I'll probably laugh out loud at having been so scared of oral surgery in the first place."

"Laugh?" snorted the nurse. "With no lips?"

* * *

Did you hear that Rubber Man married the Tattooed Lady?

By the time the honeymoon was over, he'd erased her.

* * *

George finally realized his problems were getting out of hand and made an appointment to see a psychiatrist. When he showed up, he was carrying a large round box.

"I'm glad to meet you, George," said the doctor. "As I'm sure you know, trust is at the basis of any doctor-patient relationship. Why don't you begin by showing me what's in that box?"

"Okay, doctor, if you insist," agreed George, taking off the lid. Inside sat a woman's severed head, topped by an orange felt hat covered with purple flowers.

"Oh my God!" cried the shrink, drawing back in shock. "That's grotesque."

His patient nodded in agreement. "That's just what I told her when she bought it."

* * *

What has eleven legs and summers on Cape Cod?
    Ted Kennedy's family.

* * *

Heard about the new nonprofit institution called AMD?
    It's "Mothers Against Dyslexia."

* * *

The seriously disturbed man slunk into the office of an eminent psychiatrist. "Doctor, you have to help me, it's gotten really bad," he pleaded. "I feel like nobody ever listens to me."
    The psychiatrist looked up and said, "Next!"

* * *

How many paranoid schizophrenics does it take to screw in a light bulb?
    Who wants to know?

* * *

Nine months to the day following their wedding, the Coopers had a baby. Unfortunately it was born without arms or legs—without even a torso. It was just a head. Still, the Coopers loved and cared for their child, spoiling and indulging it at every opportunity. Finally, after twenty years, they took a much-needed vacation, and whom should they meet on the cruise ship but a Brazilian doctor who had recently achieved a medical breakthrough. He promised that he could surgically attach limbs to their child and make it whole again.
    The Coopers cut their trip short, rushed home and into the room where the head lay in its crib, and cried, "Honey, Mom and Dad have a wonderful surprise for you!"
    "No," shrieked the head, "not another hat!"

* * *

Why did the man like having a midget for a girlfriend?
    Because she always wanted to go up on him.

* * *

Ramona got so horny that she finally resorted to the personal ads in her local paper. She made it quite clear that she had plenty of sensitive friends and meaningful relationships; what she was interested in was an expert lover. To put it bluntly, she wanted to get laid.
    Phone calls started coming in, with each caller testifying to his sexual prowess, but none quite struck the woman's fancy. Then one night the doorbell rang. Opening the door Ramona found

55

herself looking down at a man with no arms and no legs. "I'm terribly sorry, but the ad was very explicit," she stammered. "I'm really looking for something of a sexual athlete, and you . . . uh . . . don't have. . . . "

"Listen," interrupted her suitor, "I rang the doorbell, didn't I?"

* * *

What do you do when an epileptic has a seizure in your bathtub?
Throw in your laundry.

* * *

What's small, green, and falls apart?
A leperchaun.

* * *

This beautiful young paraplegic was sitting on the beach in her wheelchair, gazing wistfully at the crashing waves, when a handsome guy came up behind her. "Why so sad?" he asked gently.

"I've never been kissed," she replied, brushing a tear off her cheek.

"Well, I can take care of that," said the fellow. And he did, then walked off down the beach feeling pretty pleased with himself.

The next week he was strolling down the beach again when what should he see but the same lovely paraplegic, looking more down-in-the-mouth than ever. "What's wrong this time?" he asked, looking deeply into her blue eyes.

"I've never been fucked," she explained sadly.

"No problem," he declared, chest swelling with manly pride. He bent over to lift her from the wheelchair, cradled her gently in his arms, and walked slowly to the end of the pier. Tossing her into the water, he yelled down, "Now you're fucked!"

* * *

Why did the Siamese twins go to a shrink?
They were codependent.

* * *

What did the blind man say when he picked up the matzoh?
"Who wrote this?"

* * *

McEnroe, Rizzo, and Ruczek all respond to the same want ad, which requires candidates with excellent powers of observation. McEnroe is shown in first, and can't help noticing instantly that the interviewer has no ears. And when the personnel director invites him to make an observation about him, McEnroe says bluntly, "You've got no ears."

"Get out!" snarls the interviewer.

Rizzo is next. The interviewer says, "This job can only be filled by someone who is acutely observant. Make an observation about me." And when Rizzo blurts, "You've got no ears," he's shown the door.

In the waiting room Rizzo has time to warn Ruczek that the personnel director has no ears, but for God's sake not to mention the fact. So when Ruczek in turn is invited to make an observation about the interviewer, he stares at him for a minute, then says, "You're wearing contact lenses."

"Excellent," comments the interviewer, beaming. "How could you tell?"

"It wasn't hard," admits Ruczek with a modest shrug. "After all, how could you wear glasses? You've got no ears."

* * *

This guy has a blind date, and when she comes to the door his worst fears are realized: She's a paraplegic. But being a nice guy, he takes her out to dinner and the movies, and in the movie theater it doesn't take long for things to work up to the heavy-breathing stage. Still, she's sitting in a wheelchair, and he's pretty perplexed about how to take things to the next stage—if there's going to *be* a next stage.

"Don't worry," she whispers. "Take me to the playground and I'll hang from the jungle gym."

So he does just that, and they manage to have a pretty good time. She gets a little dirty and mosquito-bitten in the process, though, and he's a little apprehensive when her father comes to the door to let her in.

"You see, sir . . . " he begins, but her father interrupts him with effusive thanks. "Don't give it another thought, young man," he says warmly. "The last three guys left her hanging there."

* * *

Graffiti in the men's room:

* * *

The nervous father-to-be was pacing outside the delivery room door when finally the doctor emerged. "Thank God!" he cried. "Is it a boy or a girl?"

"Sit down, Bob," advised the doctor. "I'm afraid I have some bad news: I'm sorry to have to tell you that your child was not born anatomically complete."

Bob's face fell, but he soon cheered up. "Well they can do amazing surgery on hermaphrodites these days, right? I'm sure it'll be able to lead a normal life."

"That's not all of it, Bob. Your child was born with no arms or legs."

Bob gasped, but then he pointed out the remarkable progress being made with artificial limbs.

The doctor patted him on the arm and nodded reassuringly. "But I'm afraid it's still not going to be easy, Bob. Your child was born with no torso. In fact, your child is only a giant ear."

Bob moaned and put his hands over in a face, but in a few minutes he'd regained his composure. "My wife is a wonderful woman, Doctor, and she and I will make the best of it somehow," he declared bravely.

"There's just one more thing, Bob. It's deaf."

* * *

Did you hear about the dyslexic who tried to commit suicide?

He threw himself behind an oncoming train.

* * *

Why is it a mistake to date a necrophiliac?

He just wants you for your body.

Then again, what's the advantage to dating one?

You can be rotten and he'll still love you.

* * *

The Personnel Director was interviewing people for a position as an account executive. One candidate offered excellent references and experience, and was well-dressed and well-spoken. The only catch was a disconcerting mannerism: The fellow couldn't seem to stop winking.

So the Personnel Director decided to be frank. "You've got all the qualifications for the job and I'd really like to hire you, but I have to be honest: I'm afraid that facial tic of yours might put clients off."

"I'm glad you brought that up, sir," said the candidate, "because all I need to make that annoying wink go away is a couple of aspirins. See for yourself, I've got some on me." And he began emptying his pockets on the desk. The prospective employer started to see dozens of packages of condoms piling up: ribbed ones, lubricated ones, multicolored ones, every variety imaginable.

"Aha," cried the young man happily, "here they are." He brandished two aspirins, swallowed them, and sure enough the wink went away in less than a minute.

"So much for the wink," said the sales manager sternly, gesturing at the mountain of rubbers, "but what about all this stuff here? I don't want the company to be represented by some wild womanizer."

"No fear. I'm a happily married man."

"So how can you account for the contents of your pockets?"

"It's quite simple, sir," the fellow assured him earnestly. "Did you ever go into a drug store, winking like crazy, and ask for a packet of aspirin?"

* * *

Did you hear about the blind gynecologist?

He could read lips.

* * *

Why don't blind people sky dive?

Because it scares the hell out of their seeing-eye dogs.

* * *

"Andrew, I'm really worried about Patty," confessed James to his best friend over the phone. "She wasn't home when I got here, she hasn't called, and it's after midnight. You know how depressed she's been since her mastectomy. . . . Think something could have happened to her?"

"Now try not to worry," soothed his buddy. "Maybe Patty went out for a drink. Maybe she's visiting a friend, know what I mean?"

James glanced at the bedside table and shook his head glumly. "I doubt it. She left her tits behind."

* * *

How do you get a one-armed Pole out of a tree?

Wave at him.

* * *

"Great news, Mr. Oscarsson," the psychiatrist reported. "After eighteen months of therapy, I can pronounce you finally and completely cured of your kleptomania. You'll never be trapped by such desires again."

"Gee, that's great, Doc," said the patient with a sigh of relief.

"And just to prove it, I want you to stop off at Sears on the way home and walk the length of the store. You'll see—you'll feel no temptation to shoplift whatsoever."

"Oh Doctor, how can I ever thank you?"

"Well," suggested the doctor, "if you do have a relapse, I could use a microwave."

* * *

Know why the Siamese twins moved to England?

So the other one could drive.

* * *

"Shep's a really nice guy, Barbara, and I'm sure you really love him, but how can you bear being married to a quadriplegic?" Cynthia marveled to her model girlfriend. "He can't even wiggle his little finger. And let's face it: With your face and your body, you could have picked just about any guy on the planet."

"You don't get it, Cyn," replied Barbara. "Who needs fingers? Shep's tongue is eight inches long."

"An eight-inch tongue?" Cynthia gasped.

"And that's not all," Barbara added smugly. "He's learned to breathe through his ears."

* * *

What do you say to a woman with no arms and no legs?

"Nice tits!"

* * *

Aunt Jean was rattling along in her Oldsmobile when she got a flat tire. Being an independent sort, she jacked up the car and undid the nuts and bolts, but as she was pulling the tire off, she lost her balance and fell backwards onto the hubcap holding the hardware. And it rolled right down into a storm sewer.

This entire incident occurred right outside the state insane asylum and happened to be observed by an inmate watching carefully through the bars. "Listen lady," he called out, "just use one bolt from each of the other three tires. They'll be plenty strong enough to get you to the gas station."

"Quick thinking," said Aunt Jean admiringly. "Now why on earth is a bright boy like you stuck in that place?"

"Lady, I'm here for being crazy, not stupid."

* * *

Why were the midget and the fat lady so deliriously happy?

She let him try out a new wrinkle every night.

LEPER

What did the leper say to the prostitute?
"Keep the tip."

* * *

What happened when the leper's Mom died?
He fell apart.

* * *

How come the leper couldn't talk?
The cat got his tongue.

* * *

Why did the leper flunk his driver's test?
He left his foot on the gas.

* * *

How can you tell when a leper's been in your shower?
The bar of soap's bigger.

* * *

How do you circumcise a leper?
Shake him.

* * *

Why didn't the leper cross the road?
He didn't have the balls.

* * *

How do lepers commit suicide?
By giving head.

* * *

What happened to the leper when he visited Times Square?
Someone stole his kneecaps.

* * *

Why is this book off limits to lepers?
    They might laugh their asses off.

* * *

What's the best thing about marrying a girl who has leprosy?
    She can only give you lip once.

* * *

How can you tell when a valentine is from a leper?
    The tongue's in the envelope.

* * *

How could you tell when the poker game at the leper colony was over?
    Someone threw his hand in.

* * *

What do you get when you screw a leper?
    A piece of ass.

* * *

What do you call a leper with AIDS?
    Trendy.

HELEN KELLER

What's Helen Keller's favorite joke?
    "What's a light bulb, and how do you screw it in?"

* * *

What's Helen Keller's idea of oral sex?
    A manicure.

* * *

Why did Helen Keller wear skintight pants?
    So people could read her lips.

* * *

How did Helen Keller pierce her ear?
    Answering the stapler.

* * *

What was the meanest present Helen Keller ever got?
    A paint-by-number set.

* * *

And what was the meanest present Helen Keller ever gave?
    Her first paint-by-number picture.

* * *

How come Helen Keller never changed her baby?
    So she always knew where to find him.

* * *

Why does Helen Keller masturbate with one hand?
    So she can moan with the other.

* * *

How did Helen Keller burn her fingers?
    Reading the waffle iron.

Scorch her ear?
>Answering the iron.

* * *

Why were Helen Keller's fingers purple?
>She heard it through the grapevine.

* * *

Why was Helen Keller's leg yellow?
>Her dog was blind, too.

* * *

What's Helen Keller's favorite color?
>Corduroy.

* * *

What did Helen Keller say when she fell off the cliff?
>Nothing—she had her gloves on.

* * *

What did Helen Keller say as she was making love with her new boyfriend?
>"Funny, you don't feel Jewish."

* * *

What was Helen Keller's worst day?
>When she burned her mouth on a slice of pizza and couldn't *taste* anything either.

* * *

Why did Helen Keller marry an African-American?
>It was easy to read his lips.

MALE ANATOMY

What was the first thing Adam said to Eve?

"Stand back—I don't know how big this thing's gonna get!"

* * *

Having married a virgin, the newlywed husband wished to go to special pains to make sure her sexual inexperience wouldn't be the cause of any trouble. Taking her into his arms that first night, he explained that he didn't ever want her to feel pressured into having sex with him, that it should always be a matter of her own free will.

"In fact, darling," he went on tenderly, "I think we should set up a little system so there will never be cause for a misunderstanding between us. Here's how it'll work: When you want to have sex, pull my penis once; when you don't want to, pull my penis a hundred times."

* * *

What did the flasher say to the woman in subzero weather?

"It's so cold—should I just describe myself?"

* * *

Hungry for company, the young couple is delighted when a spaceship lands on their isolated farm and out steps a young, very humanoid, Martian couple. They get to talking and soon the wife invites the Martians to dinner. And over dinner the conversation is so stimulating and all four get along so well that they decide to swap partners for the night.

The farmer's wife and the male Martian get the master bedroom, and when he undresses she sees that his phallus is very small indeed. "What are you going to do with that?" she can't resist asking.

"Watch," he says smartly. He twists his right ear and his penis suddenly grows to eighteen inches in length—but it's still as skinny as a pencil. And again the farmer's wife can't suppress a disparaging comment.

So the Martian twists his left ear, at which his prick grows thick as a sausage. And he and the woman proceed to screw like crazy all night long.

The next morning the Martian couple takes off after cordial farewells, and the farmer turns to his wife. "So how was it?" he asks curiously.

"It was fabulous, really out of this world," reports the wife with a big smile. "How about you?"

"Nothing special," admitted the farmer. "Kinda weird in fact. All night long she kept playing with my ears."

* * *

Did you hear about the hermaphrodite baby?

It has a penis *and* a brain.

* * *

Sergeant Mack had a fine time during his stay in Hong Kong, but paid for it when he came down with a strange venereal disease. So he made the rounds of every American doctor in the community. To his horror he discovered that not only were they unable to cure him, each informed him that the only course of treatment was to have his penis amputated.

Desperate, Sergeant Mack made an appointment with a leading Chinese doctor, figuring that he might know more about an Eastern malady. "Do you, Doctor Cheung, think I need to have my dick amputated?" he asked anxiously.

"No, no, no," said the Chinese doctor testily.

A huge smile broke out over the serviceman's face. "Boy, that's *great*, Doc. Every one of those American medics said they'd have to cut it off."

"Those Western doctors—all they ever want to do is cut, cut, cut," explained Dr. Cheung exasperatedly. "You just wait two weeks. Penis fall off all by itself."

* * *

Explaining to his doctor that his sex life wasn't all it could be, Milt asked for a pill that would enable him to get it up for his wife. It so happened that the doctor had just the right medication, so Milt took a pill and drove home. But when he got to the apartment his wife wasn't at home, and after waiting for an hour or so in growing discomfort, Milt finally had to jerk off.

When the doctor called to check in the next day, Milt explained what had happened. "Well, gee, Milt, you didn't have to do for yourself," pointed out the doctor. "There are other women in the building."

"Doctor," said Milt, "for other women I don't need a pill."

* * *

It was time for sex-education class, and the teacher asked the class, "Children, who can tell me what breasts are?"

"My mommy has breasts," piped up Rhonda, "two of them."

"Right you are," praised the teacher. "And who can tell me what a penis is?"

"Me, me," piped up Eric. "My Daddy has two of them."

"Oh, really? Are you sure about that, Eric?"

"Yup. One's about this long," the little boy told her, holding his hands about four inches apart, "and looks like mine, and the other one's about this long," holding his hands about seven inches apart, "and he uses it to brush Mommy's teeth with."

* * *

What's twelve inches long and white?

Nothing.

* * *

A young man had always been plagued with insecurities about the size of his endowment. Deciding to take matters into his own hands, he went to a doctor and announced his desire to have his penis surgically enlarged.

The doctor checked things out and informed the patient that the only real possibility was to implant a section of baby-elephant trunk.

Rather radical, agreed the young man, but he was adamant in his desire to proceed, whatever the risk. The surgery went off without a hitch, and after a month of recuperation, the man decided it was time to try out his new equipment in the field.

He asked a lovely young woman of his acquaintance out to dinner at an elegant restaurant. They were enjoying appetizers and quiet conversation when his new organ, which had been comfortably resting in his left pants leg, whipped out over the table, grabbed a hard roll, and just as speedily disappeared from sight.

"Wow!" exclaimed his date, clearly impressed. "Can you do that again?"

"Sure," answered the fellow, "but I don't know if my asshole can take another hard roll."

* * *

What's the difference between light and hard?
1) It's light all day.
2) You can sleep with a light on.

* * *

One day Fred and George went out hunting. After a while George had to take a leak, and was relieving himself behind a bush when a poisonous snake lunged out and bit him right on his dick. Hearing his buddy's howl of pain, Fred told him to lie still while he rushed into town for help.

The nearest doctor told the breathless Fred that there was only one way to save his friend's life. "If you cut an *X* across the bite and suck all the poison out, he'll probably make it. Otherwise there's not much hope."

Hearing Fred's footsteps returning through the undergrowth, George rose weakly on one elbow and cried out, "Fred, what'd he say? What did the doctor say?"

"George, old pal," replied Fred sadly, "he said you're gonna die."

* * *

What's true in baseball as well as sex?
Nice guys finish last.

* * *

Two drinking buddies made a night of it. As they closed the last bar in town, one admitted to the other, "God I hate getting in at this hour. All I want to do is take my shoes off and crawl into bed, but Marge always wakes up and nags the shit out of me for what seems like hours."

"Sneaking's not the way to do it," advised his buddy conspiratorially as they staggered arm in arm down the sidewalk. "Try slamming the front door, stomping upstairs, and yelling, 'Hey baby, let's fuck.' My wife always pretends she's sound asleep."

* * *

70

Why does a dog lick his balls?

Because he can.

* * *

After a few years of marriage, Maryanne became increasingly dismayed by her diminishing sex life. She tried everything she could think of, from greeting her husband at the door dressed in Saran Wrap to purchasing exotic paraphernalia from a mail-order sex boutique. But none of it had the desired effect on her husband's libido, and finally she persuaded him to consult a hypnotist.

Maryanne was delighted that after only a few visits, her husband's ardor was restored to honeymoon dimensions. There was only one annoying side effect: Every so often during lovemaking he would jump up and run out of the room for a minute or two. At first his wife didn't want to rock the boat, but eventually her curiosity overcame her better judgement. Following him into the bathroom, she saw him staring into the mirror, muttering, "She's not my wife. . . . She's not my wife. . . . She's not my wife. . . . "

* * *

What's the definition of a sensitive guy?

A man who doesn't make his girlfriend go down on him after he screws her up the ass.

* * *

The patient cleared his throat a little embarrassedly before explaining his rather unusual problem. "YOU SEE, DOC," he boomed in a voice so deep and raspy it was almost impossible to understand, "I CAN'T GO ON WITH THIS VOICE ANYMORE—IT'S DRIVING ME CRAZY. CAN YOU FIX IT SO I SOUND LIKE A NORMAL PERSON?"

"I'll certainly try," said the doctor. After examining the patient, he reported that some sort of weight was pulling on the vocal cords and distorting the voice. "Any idea what it could be?" he queried.

The patient cleared his throat again. "ACTUALLY DOC, I HAPPEN TO BE . . . UH . . . ESPECIALLY WELL ENDOWED, AND MAYBE THAT'S WHAT'S DOING IT. LISTEN, IF YOU HAVE TO REMOVE SOME OF IT, THAT'S FINE BY ME. I'LL DO *ANYTHING* TO GET A VOICE LIKE A REGULAR GUY." So the doctor went ahead and performed the operation.

Two weeks later the patient telephoned the doctor's office. "Hey doc," he babbled happily, "I can't thank you enough. Finally

I sound like anyone else—it's just great!" After a pause, he asked, "Say, by the way, what'd you do with the piece of my penis you removed?"

"I THREW IT AWAY," said the doctor.

* * *

The routine practice of circumcision was part of a certain small-town doctor's job, and he found himself reluctant to discard the foreskins. So he saved them all up in a jar of formaldehyde. Many years went by and the doctor decided to retire. As he was cleaning out his office he came across the jar, which by this time contained hundreds of foreskins. Again it seemed a pity to throw them away, especially after all this time. So the doctor took the jar to the tailor shop around the corner. "Say, can you make something with these?" he asked.

"No problem," replied the tailor cheerfully after assessing the contents of the jar. "Come back in a week." And a week later he proudly presented the doctor with a beautiful wallet.

"Now wait just a minute," protested the doctor. "It's very nice, but there were literally hundreds of foreskins in that jar. All I get to show for them is a measly *wallet?*"

"Calm down, Doc," the tailor said reassuringly. "Rub it a little bit and it turns into a suitcase."

* * *

What can a Lifesaver do that a man can't?

Come in five different flavors.

* * *

Edith and Roberta were hanging out their laundry in their back yards when the talk came around to why Marcia's laundry never got rained on. So when Marcia came out with her laundry basket, Roberta asked her how she managed it. "Your laundry's never hanging out on those days," she commented in an aggrieved tone.

Marcia leaned over her fence and winked at her two friends. "When I wake up in the morning I look over at Buddy," she explained. "If his penis is hanging over his right leg, I know it's going to be fair weather and I come right out with my laundry. On the other hand, if it's hanging left, for sure it's going to rain so I hang it up inside."

"Well, smarty-pants," said Edith, "what's the forecast if Buddy's got a hard-on?"

"Honey," replied Marcia with a smile, "on a day like *that* you don't do the *laundry*."

* * *

What's the definition of macho?

Jogging home from your own vasectomy.

* * *

An eight-year-old boy was charged with the rape of a grown woman, and though the charge seemed highly unlikely, the state's evidence was overwhelming. As a last, desperate move, the defense counsel came over to his client on the witness stand, pulled down his pants, and took hold of the little boy's tiny penis. "Ladies and gentlemen," the lawyer cried, gesturing towards the jury box, "surely you cannot believe that such a small, as yet undeveloped organ is sexually mature?" Growing more agitated, he went on, "How could it be capable even of erection, let alone the rape of a twenty-eight-year-old—"

"WATCH IT!" yelped the kid from the stand. "One more shake and you'll lose the case."

* * *

Jake and Jim were about to head out for a long winter trapping in the northernmost wilds of Saskatchewan. When they stopped for provisions at the last tiny town, the proprietor of the general store, knowing it was going to be a good many months without female companionship, offered them two boards featuring fur-lined holes.

"We won't be needing anything like that," Jim protested, and Jim shook his head righteously. But the storekeeper pressed the boards on them, pointing out that they could always be burned as firewood.

Seven months later, bearded and gaunt, Jake walked into the general store. After a little chitchat about the weather and the trapping, the storekeeper asked where his partner was.

"I shot the son of a bitch," snarled Jake. "Caught him dating my board."

* * *

What did the elephant say to the naked man?

"How d'you breathe through that thing?"

* * *

One day Gary went into the local tattoo parlor with a somewhat odd request. He had this great new girlfriend named Wendy, he explained, and while their sex life was dynamite, he was sure it would be even better if he had her name tattooed on his prick.

The tattoo artist did her best to dissuade him, pointing out that it would be very painful, and that most of the time the tattoo would just read WY anyway. But Gary was undeterred, and insisted on going ahead with the tattoo. Sure enough, Wendy was crazy about it, and their sex grew even wilder and more frequent. Gary was a happy man.

One day he was downtown and had to take a leak in a public bathroom. At the next urinal was a big black guy, and when Gary looked over he was surprised to see WY on this guy's penis as well. "How about that!" he exclaimed. "Say, is your girlfriend's name Wendy too?"

"No, mon," answered the black guy. "Mine says, WELCOME TO JAMAICA AND HAVE A NICE DAY."

* * *

Ohrenstein was less than pleased with the doctor's remedy for the constant fatigue that was plaguing him. "Give up sex completely, Doctor?" he screamed. "I'm a young guy. How can you expect me to just go cold turkey?"

The doctor scratched his chin. "So get married and taper off gradually."

* * *

Did you hear about the guy who got his vasectomy at Sears?

Every time he gets a hard-on, the garage door goes up.

* * *

Jack was delighted by the opportunity to use the golf course at the swank country club, and even more so when he hit a hole-in-one on the eighth hole. As he bent over to take his ball out of the cup, a genie popped out. "This club is so exclusive that my magical services are available to anyone who hits a hole-in-one on this hole," the genie explained. "Any wish you desire shall be granted."

"How about that!" Jack was thrilled, and immediately requested a longer penis.

"Your wish is granted," intoned the genie solemnly, and disappeared down the hole in a puff of incense.

The golfer went on down the green, and as he walked, he could feel his dick slowly lengthening. As the game progressed, Jack could feel it growing and growing, down his thigh, out from his shorts leg, down past his knee. "Maybe this wasn't such a great plan after all," muttered Jack to himself, and headed back to the eighth hole with a bucket of balls. Finally he managed a hole in one, and when he went to collect the ball, he had to hold up the head of his dick to keep it from dragging on the ground.

Out popped the genie. "This club is so exclusive that my magical services are available to anyone who hits a hole-in-one on this hole. Any wish you—"

"Yeah, yeah, yeah," interrupted Jack. "Could you make my legs longer?"

* * *

As he got into bed the husband was very much in the mood, but was hardly surprised when his wife pushed his hand off her breast. "Lay off, honey. I have a headache."

"Perfect," he responded, without missing a beat. "I was just in the bathroom powdering my dick with aspirin."

* * *

Two none-too-bright ranch hands went into Sacramento for a wild night. They took two obliging hookers back to their hotel room, where things proceeded to heat up. At this point the girls provided them with condoms, explaining that they were protection against AIDS, VD, and herpes.

A couple of hours after the girls had left, one ranch hand poked the other. "Sal," he asked sleepily, "do you really care if those girls get VD?"

"Naw," Sal mumbled.

"So let's take these damn things off—I have to take a wicked piss!"

* * *

One day a mouse was driving along the road in his Mercedes when he heard an anguished roar from the side of the road. Pulling over, he got out and discovered a lion stuck in a deep ditch and roaring for help. The mouse obligingly tied a rope around the axle of the Mercedes, threw the other end down to the mighty beast, and pulled the lion out. The big cat thanked the mouse profusely and the two animals went their separate ways.

Two weeks later the lion was out for a stroll when he heard panicked squeaks coming from the side of the road. What should he come across but the same mouse, stuck in the same ditch. "Oh please help me, Mr. Lion," squealed the terrified rodent. "I saved you with my car, remember?"

"Of course I'll help you, little feller," the lion assured him. "I'm just going to lower my dick down to you, you hold on to it, and we'll have you out of there in a jiffy." Sure enough, in a matter of moments the mouse was high and dry on the roadside, trying to convey his eternal gratitude to the lion.

"Don't give it another thought," said the lion graciously. "It just goes to show that if you've got a big dick, you don't need a Mercedes."

* * *

A little girl walked into the bathroom, saw her father in the shower, and ran to her mother screaming, "Mommy, Mommy! Daddy has a big ugly worm hanging out of his weewee!"

"That isn't a worm, sweetheart," said her mother reassuringly. "That's part of your daddy's body and a very important part. If your daddy didn't have one of those, you wouldn't be here. And come to think of it . . . neither would I."

* * *

Casey made an appointment with a sex therapist and explained that he and his wife were unable to achieve simultaneous climax. "It's not a terrible problem, Doctor," he conceded, "but isn't there something I could do about it?"

The therapist confided that he and his wife had had the same problem, which he'd solved by hiding a pistol under his pillow. "When I was about to come, I reached for the gun and fired a shot, and Doreen climaxed with me. Come back next week and tell me how it works for you."

That very night the therapist got a call from the county hospital and rushed over to the emergency room. "What happened, Casey?" he cried, catching sight of his patient writhing in pain on an examining table, clutching a bloodsoaked towel to his groin.

Wincing, Casey explained that he'd gone right out to purchase a .45, hid it under the pillow, and started making love to his wife. "And when I was about to come, I grabbed the gun and fired."

"So?" pursued the doctor.

"She shat in my face and bit off the end of my dick."

* * *

Did you hear about the gay man who wore absolutely nothing to the costume party except for roller skates?

He went as a pull toy.

* * *

It's late at night when a spaceship lands in the middle of nowhere in central Iowa. The aliens—who look kind of like your average gas pump, not exactly but pretty close—descend from the ship and begin looking for signs of intelligent life. Coming across a road, they follow it until they come across a gas station with one pump, which looks somewhat like an alien—not exactly, but pretty close.

The captain is overjoyed—this must be what they are seeking! Deciding to make contact, he intones to the pump, "Greetings. We come from planet Xjbzoldt. Will you take us to your leader?" When there's no response, he repeats his query as loudly as possible. Still no answer, so he turns to his voice translator. Finally, enraged by the lack of a reply, he whips out his laser gun and points it at the pump. "You insolent son of a whore—take us to your leader or I'll blast you!" His lieutenant tries to stop him, but it's too late. The captain fires, and an immense explosion hurls the aliens a hundred feet in the air.

Three hours later they come to. In a shaky voice the captain asks, "Wha . . . what happened?"

The lieutenant replies, "Look captain, if I've told you once, I've told you a hundred times: You just don't go messing with a guy who can wrap his prick twice around his waist and stick it in his ear."

* * *

A well-dressed man walked into a bar in a small town. Ordering two martinis, he downed one and carefully poured the other one over his hand. After he'd done this a second time, the bartender couldn't restrain himself. "I hope you don't mind me asking, sir, but why are you wasting those drinks?"

The man smiled wanly and explained, "Just getting my date drunk."

* * *

Did you hear about the homely guy who finally got a blind date?

He put sunglasses on his inflatable sex doll.

* * *

Harry dropped by his fiancée's apartment unexpectedly one evening and told her he had to break off their engagement. "There's another woman," he said shamefacedly.

Once her hysterical sobs had subsided, Suzanne turned on him. "What does this other woman have that I don't," she demanded. "Can she cook all your favorite dishes like I do?"

"Nope. She can't boil water," Harry admitted.

"Does she spend her money buying you presents and taking you to nice restaurants?" Suzanne demanded.

"Nope. She's never reached for the check in her life," Harry said glumly.

"Then it must be sex." Suzanne broke into fresh tears.

Harry shook his head sadly. "You're the best lover I've ever had."

"Then what *can* she do that I can't?"

"Sue me for child support."

* * *

What's the definition of a faithful husband?

One whose alimony checks never bounce.

* * *

Two businessmen meet on the evening commuter train and get to talking. Pretty soon the subject comes around to their wives. Says Fred, "You should know that my wife is actually pretty ugly."

"She may not be a beauty," says Phil, "but my wife is probably the ugliest woman on the face of the Earth."

They argue back and forth about whose wife is uglier, until Fred resolves the dispute. "You come home with me right now, Phil, and meet my wife. If you still think yours is uglier, we'll go over to your house to check her out." So off they go to Fred's, where they say hello to his wife and then step outside. "Well?" asks Fred smugly.

"Your wife is plenty homely," concedes Phil, "but mine has her beat cold." He drives a skeptical Fred over to his house, leads him in the back door, slides open a trap door, and yells, "Honey, come on up."

"Okay," a woman's voice calls back. "Should I put the bag over my head?"

"No," yells Phil, "I don't want to screw you, I just want to show you to somebody."

* * *

Todd's topics of conversation had always been limited to work and sports, and once he retired he spent every waking minute attending games, glued to the sports channel, or reading *Sports Illustrated*. At first Shirley was glad he had a hobby to keep him busy, but his obsession grew irritating, and eventually infuriating.

One night as they lay in bed together, Todd glued to a Rumanian soccer match, Shirley decided she'd had enough. She got up, walked across the room, and unplugged the television.

"Hey, what do you think you're doing?" he protested.

"Listen to me, Todd," she screeched. "I'm *sick* of sports. You've barely talked to me in weeks, not to mention actually touching me. We need to have a talk about sex."

"Uh . . . okay," agreed her startled mate. "So how often do you think Lawrence Taylor gets laid?"

* * *

What's the difference between a man and E.T.?

E.T. phoned home.

* * *

"Dr. Spiegelman, things have been just terrible since Matt's appointment with you," complained Mrs. Jenkins to her husband's internist. "I made him come in because he was having terrible headaches, and sure enough, they've gone away. But now he stays out late every night, and every time he looks at me, he makes a face like he's going to throw up or something."

"Gee, Mrs. Jenkins," said the doctor apologetically, "all I did was give him a new pair of glasses."

* * *

How do men exercise at the beach?

By sucking in their stomachs every time a bikini goes by.

* * *

What was the young man's clue that his penis was really small?

When his girlfriend went down on him, she didn't suck, she flossed.

* * *

The horny college kid borrowed his roommate's car, scraped together every penny he could find, and picked up his date at her parents' house. He grew more and more upset when she proceeded to order everything pricey on the menu: fancy mixed drinks, lobster, champagne, the works. Finally he couldn't stay silent anymore, and blurted, "Does your mother feed you like this at home?"

"Nope," she replied with a demure smile, "but my Mom's not trying to get laid either."

* * *

Did you hear about the well-meaning guy who went to a Premature Ejaculators Anonymous meeting but nobody was there?

He was an hour early.

* * *

What's Niagara Falls?

A bride's second greatest disappointment.

* * *

Henderson was cruising along at fifty-five mph when to his surprise he spotted a motorcycle cop gesturing for him to pull over.

"It's your wife," explained the cop as soon as Henderson had come to a stop. "She fell out of the car five miles back."

"Thank God," Henderson exclaimed in relief. "I thought I'd gone deaf!"

* * *

How can you tell if a guy's a real loser?

When he calls a porn service and the girl says, "Not tonight, I've got an earache."

* * *

The innocent hick decided to make the long trip into town and find himself a nice girl to settle down with. Without too much trouble he found a willing woman at the corner bar and off they went to the Justice of the Peace. He rented a room in a hotel on Main Street, they screwed all night long, and the farm boy went to sleep a happy man.

But the next morning his new bride woke up to the sound of her husband, sitting bolt upright in bed, sobbing his heart out.

"What's wrong, honey?" she asked.

"One night," he moaned, "and it's all used up."

* * *

The handsome construction worker considered himself quite the stud, and indeed had no trouble persuading a good-looking recent acquaintance to come back to his apartment. After making love to her, he rolled over and lit a cigarette. His self-satisfied smile vanished, however, when the woman hopped out of bed and snapped, "You may look like Mel Gibson, but you're lousy in the sack."

The indignant fellow snapped, "I don't see what makes you such an expert after only forty-five seconds!"

* * *

Why's beauty more important than brains for a woman?

Because plenty of men are stupid, but not very many are blind.

* * *

The only survivor of a shipwreck, Pierre washed ashore on a desert island. He managed to find food and water, and didn't mind the solitude, but he grew horny as hell, so when a sheep walked down the beach one day, he grabbed it. Pierre led the beast back to his hut, but just as he was starting to get it on, a dog ran out of the jungle and began to attack him. And in trying to beat the dog away, Pierre had to let the sheep go.

In the weeks that followed the sheep appeared regularly, but every time Pierre tried to get romantic with her, the dog materialized and attacked him viciously.

A few months later a lovely young woman washed up on the shore. She was half drowned, but Pierre was able to resuscitate her, and when she came to, she was grateful beyond words. "You saved my life," she sobbed, "I would have drowned. How may I repay you? I'll do anything, just name it. . . . Anything!"

Pierre promptly grabbed the sheep and commanded, "Hold that dog."

* * *

"Doctor," the man told his physician, "I need a new penis."

The doctor took the request completely in stride. "No problem," he told his patient. "We have a five-incher, a seven-and-a-half-inch model, and a nine-incher. Which do you think would be right for you?"

"The nine-incher," the man decided on the spot. "But would it be possible to take a look at it first?"

"Of course," said the doctor obligingly.

"Gee, Doc," asked the patient after a few moments, "don't you have it in white?"

* * *

Did you hear the Men's Health Collective finally published a companion volume to *Our Bodies, Ourselves*?

It's called *My Dick, My Dick*.

* * *

Marvin was desperate to have sex with his girlfriend, but mortified at the prospect of revealing the very small dimensions of his penis. But finally one night he had a couple of drinks, took her out to dinner and the movies, came back to his place, and turned off the lights. After a furious make-out session, he took a deep breath, unzipped his fly, and put his dick in her hand.

"Sorry, I don't smoke," she whispered.

* * *

Why did God create men?

Because you can't teach a vibrator to mow the lawn.

* * *

Mrs. Harris went into the grocery store and asked for cat food. "You don't have a cat," the grocer pointed out. "Why do you need cat food?"

"It's for my husband's lunch," she explained coolly.

The grocer was shocked. "You can't feed your husband cat food. It'll kill him!"

"I've been giving it to him every day for a week now, and he loves it," she replied. And Mrs. Harris kept buying cat food.

One day the grocer happened to be scanning the obituary column when he noticed that Mr. Harris had passed away. When the new widow came by a few days later, he said, "I'm sorry to hear about your husband—but I told you that if you kept on feeding him cat food it would kill him."

"It wasn't the cat food that killed him," she snapped. "He broke his neck trying to lick his ass."

* * *

Why do men have more brains than dogs?

So they won't hump women's legs at cocktail parties.

FEMALE ANATOMY

What do you call a woman who can suck a golf ball through fifty feet of garden hose?

Darling.

* * *

The night before her wedding Maria pulled her mother aside for an intimate little chat. "Mom," she confided, "I want you to tell me how I can make my new husband happy."

The bride's mother took a deep breath. "Well, my child," she began, "when two people love, honor, and respect each other, love can be a very beautiful thing."

"I know how to fuck, Mom," interrupted the girl. "I want you to teach me how to make lasagna."

* * *

Why did God create women?

Because sheep can't cook.

What was another reason?

He couldn't get sheep to do windows either.

* * *

Hear about the new, all-women delivery service?

It's called UPMS—they deliver whenever the fuck they feel like it.

* * *

Three young women have all been working eighty-hour weeks for six years in the struggle to make partner at the prestigious law firm, and the cutoff date is fast approaching. Each one is brainy, talented, and ambitious, but there's only room for one new partner. At a loss as to which one to pick, the senior officer finally devises a little test. One day, while all three are out to lunch, he places an envelope containing five hundred dollars on each of their desks.

The first woman returns the envelope to him immediately.

The second woman invests the money in the market and returns fifteen hundred dollars to him the next morning.

The third woman pockets the cash.

So which one gets the promotion?

The one with the big tits!

* * *

Define the perfect woman:

A deaf, dumb, and blind nymphomaniac who owns a liquor store.

* * *

What's a perfect "10"?

A woman about waist-high with no teeth and a flat head you can put your drink on.

So what's a "Cinderella 10"?

A woman who sucks and fucks till midnight and then turns into a pizza and a six-pack.

* * *

With one look at his voluptuous new patient, all the gynecologist's professional ethics went right out the window. Instructing her to undress completely, he began to stroke the soft skin of her inner thigh. "Do you know what I'm doing?" he asked softly.

"Checking for any dermatological abnormalities, right?"

"Right," crooned the doctor, beginning to fondle her breasts and gently pinch her nipples. "And now?"

"Looking for any lumps that might be cancerous."

"Right you are," reassured the doctor, placing her feet in the stirrups, pulling out his cock, and entering her. "And do you know what I'm doing now?"

"Yup," she said, looking down. "Catching herpes."

* * *

Why is masturbation better than having sex with a man?

You know who you're dealing with.

You don't have to wait till it's hard again.

You know when you've had enough.

And you don't have to lie about how good it was.

* * *

How do you know a girl is too fat?

Young lovers try to carve their initials in her leg.

* * *

Why is swapping sex partners not such a good idea for women?

It's *sooooo* depressing when you get your husband back.

* * *

How many feminists does it take to change a light bulb?

Three. One to screw it in, one to lecture about how the socket is being exploited, and one to wish secretly that she was the socket.

* * *

What's the difference between a bitch and a slut?

A slut sleeps with everyone; a bitch sleeps with everyone except *you*.

* * *

What's the definition of a housewife?

An attachment that a husband screws on the bed to get the housework done.

* * *

It was a hot summer day in the ghetto, and a bunch of little kids were sitting out on the front stoop with no money, nowhere to go, nothing to do. Finally Curtis's father stuck his head out the window, tossed his kid two bucks, and told the kids to get lost.

Curtis dashed off down the block, the others following after him, and they were very surprised when he disappeared into the corner drugstore. In a few minutes he emerged carrying a small brown bag. "What's in the bag?" clamored his friends, crowding around him eagerly.

They were less than pleased when he pulled out a box of Tampax. "Hey, man," they groaned collectively, "we wanted to go out an' buy ourselves a good time with that money. What'd you buy *that* shit fo'?"

Curtis pointed to the box with a big smile. "It says right here on the box: You can go swimming, you can go horseback riding . . . "

* * *

85

What do you call an anorexic with a yeast infection?

A quarter-pounder with cheese.

* * *

What's the difference between garbage and a girl from New Jersey?

Sometimes garbage gets picked up.

* * *

Did you hear about the prostitute with a degree in psychology?

She'll blow your mind.

* * *

Did you hear about the poll conducted during National Orgasm Week?

Unfortunately, nine out of ten responders only pretended to celebrate.

* * *

Eager to make her mark in the world of business, the attractive new MBA took a job as executive assistant to the middle-aged owner of a fast-growing computer software company. She found the work challenging and the travel interesting, but was extremely annoyed by her boss's tendency to treat her in public as though she were his girlfriend rather than a professional associate.

This was especially irritating in restaurants, where he would insist on ordering for her, and on calling her "dearest" or "darling" within earshot of the waiters. When she told him how much it bothered her, he promised to stop, but the patronizing behavior continued. Finally, as he led her into a four-star restaurant, she took matters into her own hands.

"Where would you like to sit, sweetheart?" he asked, with a wink at the maitre d'.

"Gee," she replied, "anywhere you say, Dad."

* * *

How can you tell when a woman's cooking is really lousy?

Natives come from the Amazon to dip their arrows in it.

* * *

Ever realize that Ginger Rogers did everything Fred Astaire did . . .

. . . only backwards and in high heels?

* * *

How do you get a blond to say "No"?

Me either.

* * *

The gynecologist stuck up his head after completing his examination. "Removing that vibrator's going to be tricky, but I'm pretty sure I can manage it."

"Don't knock yourself out," said the woman cheerfully. "Why don't you just replace the batteries?"

* * *

Why's the new contraceptive sponge such a great idea?

Because after sex your wife can get up and wash the dishes.

* * *

Mrs. Brunckhorst went into surgery for a routine breast biopsy, and when she came to, she found the doctor standing by her bed.

"I've got some bad news and some good news," he said, taking her hand comfortingly in his. "I'm afraid we found malignant tumors in both breasts, and had to remove both of them completely."

"Oh my God," said the poor woman, bursting into tears.

"There, there, don't forget the good news," the surgeon reminded her.

"What could that be?" she sobbed.

"The transvestite in the next bed wants to buy all your old bras."

* * *

How can you tell if your girlfriend's too fat?

If she sits on your face and you can't hear the stereo.

* * *

The real-estate mogul was delighted by the comely new receptionist, and proceeded to turn all of his charms upon her. Within a few weeks, however, he grew extremely displeased at her growing tardiness. "Listen, baby," he roared one morning, "we may have gone to bed together a few times, but who said you could start coming in late?"

The secretary replied sweetly, "My lawyer."

* * *

What are three things a woman can do that a man can't?

1. Have a period.
2. Have a baby.
3. Get laid when she's dead.

* * *

And what are the three best things about being a woman?

You can bleed without cutting yourself;

You can bury a bone without digging a hole;

And you can make a man come without calling him.

* * *

This woman goes to the gynecologist for the first time and is rather embarrassed as she puts her feet in the stirrups. The doctor goes around for a look and says, "Why that's the biggest pussy I've ever seen—the biggest pussy I've ever seen!"

"You didn't have to say it twice," snaps the woman.

"I didn't," says the doctor.

* * *

How can you tell when a woman is horny?

When you put your hand in her pants and it feels like a horse eating oats.

* * *

Why don't women have brains?

They don't have a dick to put them in.

* * *

One night little Johnny walked in on his parents while they were screwing. "Daddy," he cried, "what are you and Mommy doing?"

"Uh . . . we're making a little sister for you to play with," stammered his father.

"Oh, neat," said Johnny, and went back to bed.

The next day his dad came home to find the little boy sobbing his eyes out on the front porch. "What's wrong, Johnny?" he asked, picking him up.

"You know the little sister you and Mommy made me?"

"Yes," said his father, blushing.

The little boy wailed, "Today the milkman ate it."

* * *

What's the difference between pussy and cunt?

A pussy is soft, warm, inviting . . . and a cunt is the person who owns it.

* * *

Leonard desperately wanted to become a doctor and had really crammed for his medical boards, so he wasn't in the least fazed by the question: "Name the three advantages of breast milk."

Quickly he wrote 1) It contains the optimum balance of nutrients for the newborn child. He added 2) As it is contained within the mother's body, it is protected from germs and helps develops the child's immune system. Then Leonard was stumped. Racking his brains until he'd broken a sweat, he finally scribbled 3) It comes in such nice containers.

* * *

Why's divorce a good thing?

If it weren't for divorce, where would coffee shops get their waitresses?

* * *

Two law partners can't resist hiring a gorgeous young receptionist, and despite promises to the contrary, neither can resist going to bed with her. And not too long afterwards their worst fears are realized: the blushing receptionist announces that she's pregnant. No one knows who the father is, and the partners are in a total quandary. So towards the end of the pregnancy they decide to chip in and send the girl off to Florida to have the baby.

Several months go by with no news, and finally one of the partners feels so guilty that he hops on a flight to go check on the young mother. The next night the phone rings in their New York office.

"How is she?" asks his partner.

"Oh, she's fine," was the breezy answer, "but I've got some bad news and some good news."

"Oh yeah? What's the good news?"

"Well, like I said, Jeannette's fine. And she had twins."

"So what's the bad news?" asked the partner from New York.

"Mine died."

* * *

Why do women have legs?

So they don't leave tracks like snails.

* * *

What's the definition of eternity?

The length of time between when *you* come and *she* leaves.

* * *

Three guys were sitting around in a bar one afternoon discussing whose wife was the most frigid. Harry was positive he had the worst of it. "Listen, you guys, my wife comes to bed with an ice cube in each hand, and in the morning they haven't begun to melt."

"That's *nothing*," said Phil. "My wife likes to have a glass of water on the bedside table, but by the time she's carried it in from the bathroom, it's frozen solid."

"Aw, hell," snorted Herb, "*my* wife is so frigid that when she spreads her legs, the furnace kicks on."

* * *

Why does it take women longer to climax?

Who cares?

* * *

A nymphomaniac goes to the supermarket and gets all hot and bothered eyeing the carrots and cucumbers. By the time she gets to the checkout line she can't hold out much longer, so she asks one of the supermarket baggers to carry her groceries out to the car for her. They're halfway across the lot when the nympho slips her hand down his pants and whispers, "You know, I've got an itchy pussy."

"Sorry, lady," says the bagger, "but I can't tell one of those Japanese cars from another."

* * *

What do fat girls and mopeds have in common?

They're both fun to ride until a friend sees you.

* * *

What's the difference between a hormone and an enzyme?

You can't hear an enzyme.

* * *

"Say," said Lucille one day over lunch, "weren't you going to go out with that guy who played the French horn?"

"Yeah," said Diane, stirring her ice tea. "He was a pretty nice guy. But there was one real problem . . . "

"Oh, really?"

"Every time he kissed me, he wanted to shove his fist up my ass."

* * *

Why don't they let women swim in the ocean any more?

They can't get the smell out of the fish.

* * *

After going through Lamaze, Leboyer, and LaLeche classes with his expectant wife, the proud new father remained by his wife's side throughout labor and birth, bonding with the newborn. Wanting to share the experience as much as possible, he took his wife's hand and said, "Tell me, darling, how did it actually feel to give birth?"

His wife replied. "Okay. Smile as hard as you can."

Beaming down at his wife and child, the fellow commented, "That's not too hard."

She went on, "Now stick your fingers in the corners of your mouth." He obeyed, still smiling broadly.

"Now stretch your lips as hard as you can," she instructed.

"Still not too tough," he commented.

"Right. Now pull them over your head."

* * *

Why is a clitoris like Antarctica?

Most men know it's there but they don't really care.

* * *

A certain couple fell on really hard times, and since the husband already worked full-time and part of a night shift, they decided the only way to keep the family afloat was for the wife to sell her body.

One night she went out and didn't return until the wee hours, disheveled and exhausted. Watching her flop onto the sofa like a limp dishrag, her husband said sympathetically, "You look like you've really had a rough night, honey."

"I sure have," she gasped.

"Well, did you make a lot of money at least?" he asked.

His wife managed a proud smile. "One hundred and thirty dollars and twenty-five cents."

"Twenty-five cents!" exclaimed the husband. "Who was the cheap bastard who only gave you two bits?"

"Why," said the woman, "*all* of them."

* * *

What's the ultimate in embarrassment for a woman?

When her Ben-Wa balls set off the metal detector at the airport.

* * *

Susie was desperate for her new husband to go down on her. After everything from subtle innuendos to outright begging had failed, one night she finally resorted to trickery. "Honey," she called breathily from the bedroom, "can you help me a sec? I've got a tampon stuck inside me. I'm sure you can get it out if you use your teeth."

Disgusted, the husband pulled the diamond engagement ring off her finger and pushed it way up inside her.

"Owww!" yelped the young bride. "What did you do *that* for?"

"You really expect me to go poking around down there," snarled her husband, "for a lousy tampon?"

* * *

Why do women have two sets of lips?

So they can piss and moan at the same time.

* * *

God has just spent six days creating the heavens and the Earth, and since it's the seventh day, He and Gabriel are sitting back and admiring His handiwork.

"You know, God," says Gabriel, "you've done one hell of a job— pardon my language. Those snowy peaks are unbelievably majestic, and those woods, with their little sunny dells and meadows . . . masterful. Not to mention the oceans: those fantastic coral reefs, and all the sea creatures, and the waves crashing on pristine beaches. And all the animals, from fleas to elephants, what vision! Not to mention the heavens; how could I leave them out? What a touch, that Milky Way."

God beams.

"If you'll excuse my presumption," Gabriel goes on, "I have just the teeniest question. You know those sample humans you put down in the Garden of Eden?"

God nods, a frown furrowing His divine brow.

"Well I was just wondering whether, for the obvious reason, they shouldn't have differing sets of genitalia, the way all the other animals do?"

After God reflects on the matter for a minute or two, a big smile crosses His face. "You're absolutely right," He agrees. "Give the dumb one a cunt!"

* * *

Know how these days everyone wants a second opinion?

Well, this lady had been going to a psychiatrist for years, and one day she decided she'd had enough of it. Walking into his office, she announced, "Doctor, I've been seeing you every Thursday for five years now. I don't feel any better, I don't feel any worse. What's the story? I want you to level with me—what's wrong with me?"

"Okay, I'll tell you," said the doctor. "You're crazy."

"Now wait just a minute," protested the woman. "I'm entitled to a second opinion."

"Okay," offered the doctor obligingly. "You're ugly, too."

* * *

Did you hear why Polish women don't use vibrators?

They chip their teeth.

* * *

Why do women have two holes?

So that when they're drunk you can carry them home like a six-pack.

* * *

What's red and has seven little dents in it?

Snow White's cherry.

* * *

A young man was brought up by his father in the Australian outback. Not wanting the boy to get into trouble, the father told him to stay away from women. "They have teeth down there," he explained, and let the impressionable young boy's imagination do the rest.

Eventually, however, the old man died, and seeing his acquaintances getting married and starting families, the young man decided it was time to get on with it. So he rode into the nearest town and found himself a willing girl—who was rather disappointed when the consummation of their wedding night consisted of a peck on the cheek. The second night she dolled herself up in a sheer negligee, only to have her new husband again kiss her on the cheek, roll over, and fall fast asleep. On the third night she caught him before the snores began and proceeded to give him a brief lecture on the birds and the bees and his conjugal duties.

"Oh, no you don't!" he cried, sitting up in alarm and pulling the bedclothes tightly around himself. "I know about you women! You've got teeth down there, and I'm not coming anywhere near."

Being a good-humored sort, his bride roared with laughter,

then invited her husband to come around and see for himself. Warily he circled the bed and proceeded to check out her anatomy with great care. Finally he stuck his head up.

"You're right," he proclaimed. "You've got no teeth, and your gums are in terrible condition!"

* * *

What do you get when you cross an elephant and a prostitute?

A hooker who does it for peanuts and won't ever forget you.

* * *

Did you hear about the bride who was so horny she carried a bouquet of batteries?

* * *

"I do happen to need somebody," admitted the owner of the hardware store to the unimpressive-looking man who was interested in a job. "But tell me, can you sell?"

"Of course," was the confident reply.

"I mean really *sell*," reiterated the shopkeeper.

"You bet," said the young man.

"I'll show you what I mean," said the owner, going over to a customer who had just walked in and asked for grass seed. "We're having a very special sale on lawn mowers," he told the customer. "Could I interest you in one?"

"What do I need a lawn mower for?" protested the customer. "I don't even have any grass yet."

"Maybe not," said the owner agreeably, "but all that seed's going to grow like crazy some day and then you'll need a lawn mower in the worst way. And you won't find them on sale in mid-summer, that's for sure."

"I guess you've got a point," admitted the fellow. "Okay, show me what you've got in lawnmowers."

"Think you can do that?" asked the storekeeper of his new employee after he'd written up the bill. The man nodded. "Okay, good. Now I have to run to the bank. I'll only be gone for a few minutes, but while I'm gone I want you to sell, sell, sell."

The new guy's first customer was a woman who came over and asked where the tampons were.

"Third aisle over, middle of the second shelf."

When she came to the counter to pay, he leaned over and said, "Hey, you wanna buy a lawn mower? They're on sale."

"Why on earth would I want a lawn mower?" she asked, eyeing him suspiciously.

"Well, you aren't going to be screwing," he blurted, "so you might as well mow the lawn."

* * *

Why do tampons have strings?

So you can floss after you eat.

* * *

This guy walked into a bar and said to the bartender, "I'll have a scotch and soda . . . and get that douche bag whatever she'd like, on me." He motioned at a young woman sitting at the far end of the bar.

"Listen buddy," said the bartender, "this is a family place, and I'll thank you not to use that sort of language in here."

"Right, right," said the customer. "Just get me that scotch and soda and get the douche bag a drink."

"Now see here," sputtered the bartender, "that's a perfectly nice girl, and—"

"I'm getting thirsty," interrupted the guy, "and hurry up with the douche bag's order, too."

Giving up, the bartender walked over to the young woman and rather shamefacedly said, "The gentleman over there would like to offer you a drink—what'll you have?"

She looked up with a smile and answered, "Vinegar and water, please."

* * *

What would be one of the advantages of electing a woman president?

We wouldn't have to pay her as much!

* * *

How do you make a hormone?

Don't pay her.

* * *

Who enjoys sex more, the man or the woman?

The woman.

How can I prove it?

When your ear itches and you put your little finger in and wiggle it around and take it out again, what feels better, your finger or your ear?

* * *

The first astronaut to land on Mars was delighted to come across a beautiful Martian woman stirring a huge pot over a campfire. "Hi there," he said casually. "What're you doing?"

"Making babies," she explained, looking up with a winsome smile.

Horny after the long space voyage, the astronaut decided to give it a shot. "That's not the way we do it on Earth," he informed her.

"Oh, really?" The Martian woman looked up from her pot with interest. "How do your people do it?"

"Well, it's hard to describe," he conceded, "but I'd be glad to show you."

"Fine," agreed the lovely Martian maiden, and the two proceeded to make love in the glow of the fire. When they were finished, she asked, "So where are the babies?"

"Oh, they don't show up for another nine months," explained the astronaut.

"So why'd you stop stirring?"

* * *

Although he was skeptical about her powers, one day Eric decided to pay a call on the fortune-teller whose window he walked past every day. He sat down in front of her crystal ball and she proceeded to stare into it in deep concentration. Finally she pronounced firmly, "You are the father of two children."

"That's what you think," replied Eric smugly. "I'm the father of two boys and a girl."

The fortune-teller looked him in the eye. "That's what *you* think."

* * *

Hear about the guy who mowed the lawn with his shirt off and his back got stiff?

Now his wife wants him to mow the lawn with his pants off.

* * *

A guy walked into a bar and ordered a drink. After downing it, he sneaked a quick look in his pants pocket. After watching this maneuver six or seven times, the bartender got curious and asked, "Hey, mister, what's in your pocket that's so interesting?"

The man looked up and explained, "It's a picture of my wife. I keep drinking till she looks good, and then I go home."

* * *

Why do bald men cut holes in their pockets?

So they can run their fingers through their hair.

* * *

Mike was touching up the paint in the bathroom one weekend when the brush slipped out of his hand, leaving a stripe across the toilet seat. So Mike painted the whole seat over and went off to a ball game.

His wife happened to get home early, went upstairs to pee, and found herself firmly stuck to the toilet seat. And at six o'clock Mike found her there, furious and embarrassed.

He was unable to dislodge her for fear of tearing the skin, so with considerable difficulty Mike managed to unscrew the seat and get her into the back seat of the car and then into a wheelchair at the county hospital. She was wheeled into a room and maneuvered, on her knees, onto an examining table. At this point the resident entered and surveyed the scene. "What do you think, Doc?" broke in the nervous husband.

"Nice, very nice," he commented, stroking his chin. "But why the cheap frame?"

* * *

Why do women have cunts?

So men will talk to them.

HOMOSEXUAL

Why were the gays the first to clear out of San Francisco after the earthquake?

They already had their shit packed.

* * *

What's the definition of a lesbian?

Just another damn woman trying to do a man's job.

* * *

How can you tell if a doctor is gay?

When he does a rectal exam, both his hands are on your shoulders.

What's another clue?

He inserts suppositiories with his teeth.

* * *

"My dildo can do anything a man can do," boasted a dyke one night in a crowded bar.

"Oh yeah?" replied a drunk at a nearby table. "Let's see your dildo get up and order another round of drinks."

* * *

Two gay partners decided they wanted to have a baby, so a lesbian friend agreed to be impregnated by sperm donation. In due course she gave birth to an eight-pound baby boy, and the men rushed to the hospital. Pressing their noses against the glass of the nursery window, they surveyed row upon row of squalling babies—except for one baby cooing softly to itself amid the chaos.

Sure enough, when they asked to see their son, it was the quiet baby whom the nurse brought over for the new fathers to ogle. "He sure is well-behaved for a newborn, isn't he?" commented one of them proudly.

"Oh, he's quiet now," responded the nurse, "but he squalls like all the rest when I take the pacifier out of his ass."

* * *

Is it better to be born black or gay?

Black, because you don't have to tell your parents.

* * *

A flaming queer sashays into the roughest truckstop on the highway with a parakeet on his shoulder. He looks around the restaurant at all the burly truckers and announces loudly, "Whichever one of you big bruisers can guess the weight of this darling parakeet gets to go home with me."

Silence falls over the truckstop. Then one of the toughest-looking guys speaks up. "That's an easy one—five hundred pounds."

The fag shrieks delightedly, "We have a winner! We have a winner!"

* * *

Why was the gay man fired from his job at the sperm bank?

For drinking on the job.

* * *

"In the center ring," cries the ringmaster, "we have Nero, the boldest and bravest animal trainer in the world. Watch, ladies and gentlemen, as he puts his head between the jaws of our man-eating lion!" The crowd roars as Nero pulls out his head unscathed.

"Now, folks, watch this!" shouts the announcer, as Nero unzips his pants and puts his prick between the giant teeth. "Don't do it!" shrieks the audience as the lion's jaws clamp shut. But without flinching Nero pulls them open and removes his unharmed penis. Wild cheers fill the arena.

When the noise dies down, the ringmaster steps forward and announces, "Ladies and gentlemen, a prize of five thousand, yes five thousand dollars, to the man in our audience who'll try that trick." His jaw drops as a small, effeminate man steps right up to the ringside. "You're going to repeat that trick in front of all these people?" he asks incredulously.

"Certainly," says the fag, "but I must tell you something first. I don't think I can open my mouth as wide as the lion did."

* * *

Why don't fags lean on baseball bats?

They're afraid it might get serious.

* * *

Two gays were having a drink at the bar when an attractive woman walked by. "Mmmmmm . . . " said one appreciatively, eyeing her up and down.

"Oh, Tom!" shrieked his horrified friend. "Don't tell me you're going straight!"

"Nothing like that," said Tom musingly. "It's just that sometimes I can't help wishing I'd been born a lesbian . . . "

* * *

What's the hardest thing about having AIDS?

Trying to convince your parents you're Haitian.

* * *

Bruce was completely smitten by a handsome man who passed him on the sidewalk, so he trailed him into a building and up to his office. What luck—the fellow happened to be a proctologist! Bruce instantly called for an appointment. But as the examination progressed, his patient's sighs of evident pleasure infuriated the doctor. His job was to cure, not to titillate, and making that perfectly clear, he tossed the patient out of his office.

But Bruce had fallen in love. Unable to keep away from the object of his desire, he soon telephoned for another appointment, assuring the doctor of a legitimate medical reason. Reluctantly the doctor agreed to see him again. Beginning his examination, he was astonished to find a long green stem protruding from the gay guy's ass, then another, and another . . .

"My God!" exclaimed the proctologist angrily, "you've got a dozen red roses stuck up your ass. I warned you not to try any funny business—"

"Read the card," gasped Bruce, "read the card!"

* * *

How do you fit four gays at a crowded bar?

Turn the stool upside down.

* * *

One night Fred came home from work and told his wife over dinner that he had just signed up with the company hockey team. Worried that he might hurt himself, his wife went out the next day to buy him a jock strap.

The effeminate sales clerk was only too happy to help her. "They come in colors, you know," he told her. "We have Virginal White, Ravishing Red, and Promiscuous Purple."

"I guess white will do just fine," she said.

"They come in different sizes, too, you know," said the clerk.

"Gee, I'm really not sure what Fred's size is," confessed his wife. So the clerk extended his pinkie.

"No, it's bigger than that."

The clerk extended a second finger.

"No, it's bigger than that," said the wife.

A third finger.

"Still bigger," she said.

When the clerk stuck out his thumb, too, she said, "Yes, that's about right."

So the clerk put all five fingers in his mouth, pulled them out, and announced expertly, "That's a medium."

* * *

How can you tell a macho homosexual at the beach?

By the shaving scars on his legs.

* * *

Farmer May died during the winter, and when it came time for spring planting, Widow May realized she couldn't do all the work herself. So she applied to the town council, only to be told that all the able-bodied farmhands had already been hired and the only two left were an ex-con and a queer. Widow May chose the queer, and was pleased to find him a steady and reliable worker.

When six weeks had gone by, the fellow asked Widow May if he could have Saturday night off to go into town. "All right," she consented, "but be back by nine o'clock."

The farmhand wasn't back until ten-thirty, and as he tiptoed up the back stairs, he heard Widow May summon him into her room, where she had been waiting up.

"Take off my shoes," she ordered. He obeyed. "Take off my dress." He did so. "Take off my slip . . . and my stockings . . . and my garter belt."

The homosexual obliged in silence.

"Now take off my bra," snapped Widow May, "and don't you ever borrow my clothes again!"

* * *

Why is AIDS a scientific miracle?

It's the only thing in the world that can change a fruit into a vegetable.

* * *

Over lunch in the hospital cafeteria, one doctor happened to mention to his colleague that he'd come across a nutritional breakthrough for his AIDS patients. "Pancakes," he explained cheerfully.

"Really?" commented his friend. "I wasn't aware that pancakes had any special nutritional value."

"They don't," went on the first doctor, "but they're so easy to slide under the door."

* * *

What's the definition of an optimist?

A homosexual with an IRA.

* * *

Phillips fancied himself quite the ladies man, so when his cruise ship went down in a storm and he found himself stranded on a desert island with six women, he couldn't believe his good fortune. They quickly agreed that each woman would have one night a week with the only man. Phillips threw himself into the arrangement with gusto, working even on his day off, but as the weeks stretched into months, he found himself looking forward to that day of rest more and more eagerly.

One afternoon he was sitting on the beach and wishing for some more men to share his duties when he caught sight of a life raft bobbing in the waves. Phillips swam out to the guy, pulled the raft to shore, and did a little jig of happiness. "You can't believe how happy I am to see you," he cried.

The new fellow eyed him up and down and cooed, "You're a sight for sore eyes, too, you gorgeous thing."

"Shit," sighed Phillips, "there go my Sundays."

* * *

How do you get hearing AIDS?

From listening to assholes.

* * *

Two lesbians were having a drink at the bar when a good-looking woman waved at them from across the room.

"Nice," commented Brenda. "I'd like to get between her legs sometime soon."

"No you wouldn't," said her companion disparagingly. "She's hung like a doughnut."

* * *

Why did the grieving homosexual masturbate into his dead lover's urn?

He wanted one last piece of ash.

* * *

Heard about the new gay sitcom?

It's called "Leave It, It's Beaver."

* * *

Beset with grief, a poor homosexual had just found out that he had AIDS. "What am I going to do?" pleaded the man after his doctor had reviewed the prognosis.

"I think you should go to Mexico and live it up. Drink the water and eat all the Mexican cuisine you can get your hands on, including raw fruits and vegetables," advised the doctor.

"Oh, God, Doc, will that cure me?"

"No," answered the doctor candidly, "but it'll teach you what your asshole is for."

* * *

What do you call a Playboy bunny who's a lesbian?

Bitch.

* * *

Brad finally worked up the courage to tell his Mother he was gay, and headed over to the beauty salon where she worked as a manicurist. Taking a deep breath, he said, "Mom, I've got something really important to tell you."

"Sure, hon. Sit down and I'll do your nails while we chat," she said.

"Uh . . . I don't know quite how to say this, but something's been bothering me for a long time now . . . and I think you should know," he stammered.

"You're gay, right?"

"Yeah, that's it," Brad blurted in relief. "How'd you know, Mom?"

"It wasn't too hard to figure out," she said calmly. "You've got shit under your fingernails."

* * *

What's a Jewish mother's dilemma?

Having a gay son who's dating a doctor.

* * *

Hear about the interior decorator who fell down the stairs and was all black-and-blue?

He committed suicide because he clashed with his drapes.

"MOMMY, MOMMY"

"Mommy, Mommy, can I lick the bowl?"
  "Shut up and flush."

* * *

"Mommy, Mommy, Dad's been run over in the street!"
  "Don't make me laugh. You know my lips are chapped."

* * *

"Mommy, Mommy, can I buy a new dress?"
  "You know it won't fit over your iron lung."

* * *

"Mommy, Mommy, why do I keep going in circles?"
  "Shut up or I'll nail your other foot to the floor."

* * *

"Mommy, Mommy, why can't I play with the other kids?"
  "Shut up and deal."

* * *

"Mommy, Mommy, why is everyone running away?"
  "Shut up and reload."

* * *

"Mommy, Mommy, what's an Oedipus complex?"
  "Shut up and kiss me."

* * *

"Mommy, Mommy, why are you moaning?"
  "Shut up and keep licking!"

* * *

"Daddy, Daddy, what's a transvestite?"
  "Shut up and unhook my bra."

CRUELTY TO ANIMALS

Hear about the new breed that's half pit bull and half collie?
   After it mauls you, it goes for help.

* * *

Did you hear K-Y jelly is coming out with all new packaging?
   They're going to have pictures of missing gerbils on the labels.

* * *

One afternoon a farmer was telling his neighbor how to screw a sheep. "The trick," he shared with his friend, "is to sneak up behind her, grab hold of her rear legs, spread 'em and lift 'em up to your dick."

   "That sounds easy enough," the other farmer said, "but how do you kiss her?"

* * *

What do you call a cow with no legs?
   Ground beef.

* * *

How can you spot where flamingoes live?
   By all the plastic Mexicans in their front yard.

* * *

A man suspects his wife of cheating on him so he goes to the pet store to shop for a parrot. He sees quite an assortment for sale for five hundred to a thousand dollars but that's a bit more than he wants to spend, so he's delighted to come across one in the corner for sale for $29.95. "How come that one's so cheap?" he asks the clerk.

   "To tell ya the truth, his dick's oversized and embarrasses the customers," is the explanation. The husband buys the bird anyway, and installs it on a perch right over the bed.

The next day the first thing he does after coming home from work is to rush upstairs. "Well, what happened today?" he demands of the bird.

"Well, the milkman came, and . . . your wife told him to come into the bedroom, and . . . they took off their clothes, and . . . got into bed," the bird informs him.

"So what happened next," demands the irate husband.

"Got me," says the parrot with a shrug. "I got hard and fell off my perch."

* * *

What did the worm say to the caterpillar?

"What'd you do to get that fur coat?"

* * *

"Daddy, what are those dogs doing?" asked little Tiffany, catching sight of two dogs across the street stuck together in the act of intercourse.

"Uh . . . one dog's hurt and the other one's helping him out, honey," explained her red-faced father hastily.

"What a fuckin' world, huh, Dad?" remarked Tiffany, looking up at him sweetly. "Just when you're down and out, somebody gives it to you up the ass."

* * *

What's meaner than a pitbull with AIDS?

The guy who gave it to him.

* * *

What goes "Hoppity . . . clank . . . hoppity . . . clank?"

The Easter Bunny with polio.

* * *

The bartender was dumbfounded when a gorilla came in and asked for a martini, but he couldn't think of any reason not to serve the beast. And he was even more amazed to find the gorilla coolly holding out a ten-dollar bill when he returned with the drink.

As he walked over to the cash register, he decided to try something. He rang up the sale, headed back to the animal, and handed it a dollar in change. Nonplussed, the gorilla just sat there sipping his martini.

110

Finally the bartender couldn't take it any more. "You know," he offered, "we don't get too many *gorillas* in here."

And the gorilla returned, "At nine bucks a drink, I'm not surprised."

* * *

"How are you and that new girlfriend getting along these days?" asked one brontosaurus of another. "Gotten any action off her yet?"

The other brontosaurus shook his head mournfully. "We went away for the weekend, I had her in the mood, and wouldn't you know it—she gets her century."

* * *

What do you get when you cross a porcupine with a tapeworm?

About ten feet of barbed wire.

* * *

What did one gerbil say to another when an obviously gay man swished into the pet store?

"Don't panic! Just turn your back and act like a dog."

* * *

The pharmacist was impressed when a fussy-looking older man came in and bought a dozen rubbers one day, and *really* impressed when he returned only a week later for another dozen. When the man asked for another dozen only a few days later, the pharmacist couldn't keep quiet any longer. "You must have the stamina of a bull," he said admiringly. "How do you manage to have so many erections?"

Clearly offended, the customer informed the pharmacist that he found the whole idea of sex repulsive and wouldn't dream of indulging in pleasures of the flesh.

"So what're you doing with all the rubbers?"

"I've trained my Yorkshire terrier to swallow them," the man explained with a dainty sniff. "Now she shits in little plastic bags."

* * *

Did you hear about the paranoid bloodhound?

He thought people were following him.

* * *

Since Mortie had grown up on a farm he was accustomed to screwing the cows, and it didn't bother his father until he turned fifteen and still didn't seem to be displaying any interest in girls. So Pa went into town and hired a beautiful prostitute for the evening.

Following his directions, she went into the barn, took off all her clothes, and went over to where the farm boy was standing on a wheelbarrow screwing a big Holstein.

"Say there, Mortie," said the woman seductively, "anything I can do for you?"

Mortie looked over at her. "Sure—you can wheel me over to the next cow."

* * *

Why do elephants drink?
It helps them forget.

* * *

What do female hippos say before sex?
"Can I be on top this time?"

How about female snails?
"Faster, faster!"

* * *

Jerry was showing his friend his bee collection when Herb pointed out that he'd better poke some holes in the top of the jar. "Otherwise they won't live through the night," he cautioned.

"Hell, what do I care," said Jerry wearily. "It's only a hobby."

* * *

Did you hear about the blind skunk who tried to rape a fart?

* * *

A young mother taking her baby to the zoo for the first time made the mistake of passing too close to the great apes. A hairy arm reached out and plucked the baby out of the stroller, and the huge mountain gorilla proceeded to eat the child before her very eyes.

A policeman arrived and spent over an hour trying to calm the hysterical woman, but nothing seemed to work. Finally he put an arm around her shoulders and tried to reason with her: "Lady, don't take it so hard. You and your husband can always have another baby."

"Like hell!" she snapped. "You think I've got nothing better to do than fuck and feed gorillas?"

* * *

A farmer was extolling the virtues of pig fucking to his neighbor and urging him to give it a try. Finally, after hours of convincing, the neighbor agreed to mount one of his sows.

"I don't know Clem," the neighbor reported, "I didn't enjoy that too much."

"No wonder Clyde," the farmer laughed, "you picked the ugliest one!"

* * *

Did you hear about the new nature movie?

It's the epic story of a dysfunctional salmon who only wanted to float downstream.

* * *

Shirley had always wanted to see Australia, so she saved up her money and went off on a two-week tour. And she'd only been there three days when she fell head over heels in love with a kangaroo. Blithely disregarding the advice of her tour guide and companions, she had an aboriginal priest perform a wedding ceremony and brought her new husband back to her house in the Midwest.

But she found that the course of new love was not without its problems, and in a few months decided to consult a marriage counselor. "Frankly, in your case it's not hard to put my finger on the heart of the problem," said the counselor almost immediately. "Besides the obvious ethnic and cultural differences between you and your husband, it's clearly going to be impossible to establish genuine lines of communication with a kangaroo."

"Oh, that's not it at all," Shirley broke in. "My husband and I communicate perfectly—except in bed. There it's nothing but hop on, hop off, hop on, hop off. . . . "

* * *

What do you do with a dog with no legs?

Take it for a drag.

* * *

The nearest customer was five stools away, but that didn't keep Josh from leaning over towards the bartender and commenting, "Geez, there's a lousy smell in here." A few minutes later he added, "It smells just like . . . shit." Puzzled by the origin of the stench, he moved closer to the other customer, and sure enough the smell worsened. "Phew, you really stink," he pointed out.

"I know," said the man apologetically. "It's because of my job." Seeing that Josh was curious, he went on, "I'm with an elephant act, and before each show I have to give the elephant an enema so he doesn't take a dump during the performance. Frankly, it's a tricky business, because I have to administer it quickly and then jump back. And sometimes I just don't move fast enough."

"Jesus," commiserated Josh, shaking his head. "How much do they pay you for this lousy job?"

"Eighty-five bucks a week," said the man cheerfully.

"You've got to be kidding. Why don't you quit?"

"*What?*" cried the man. "And get out of *show* business?!"

* * *

Why do dogs stick their noses in women's crotches?

Because they can.

* * *

"I hope you can help me, Dr. Berg," said the woman to a podiatrist. "My feet hurt me all the time."

The doctor asked her to walk down the hall and back while he observed, and when she sat back down he pointed out that she was extremely bowlegged. "Do you know if this is a congenital problem?"

"Oh no, it developed quite recently. You see, I've been screwing doggie fashion a lot."

"Well I'd recommend trying another sexual position," said the doctor, slightly taken aback.

"No way," she replied tartly. "That's the only way my Doberman will fuck."

* * *

What did one Korean shark say to the other?

"Oh, no—not airplane food again."

* * *

A none-too-bright graduate student was conducting research on the nervous system of the frog. Taking a frog out of the tank and putting it on the table, he cut off one leg and said, "Jump!" The frog jumped.

Taking the scalpel, he amputated one of the frog's front legs. "Jump!" he shouted. The frog jumped.

Amputating a third limb, the student repeated his command. Bleeding profusely, the poor frog managed a feeble lurch.

After taking his scalpel to the fourth leg, the student said, "Jump!" No response from the frog. "I said *jump!*" shouted the man again. The frog didn't move. "JUMP!" he bellowed in the ear of the inert amphibian. Finally the student decided the experiment was finished.

Taking his notebook down from the shelf, the student carefully noted, "When all limbs are amputated, it is observed that the frog goes deaf."

* * *

Bert returns from a long trip, having left his beloved cat in his brother's care. The moment he reaches a phone, he calls his brother and asks, "How's my cat?"

"Your cat's dead," is the blunt reply.

Bert is devastated. "You know how much that cat meant to me," he cries. "Couldn't you at least have broken the news to me a little more gently? Couldn't you have said something like, 'Well, you know, the cat got out of the house one day and climbed up on the roof, and the fire department couldn't get her down, and she passed away from exposure . . . or starvation . . . or something?' Why are you always so thoughtless?"

"I'm really sorry," his brother apologizes abjectly. "I'll try to do better next time, Bert."

"Okay, okay, let's try and forget about it. So how's Mom?"

His brother is silent for a moment, then stammers, "Uh . . . Mom's on the roof."

* * *

What do elephants use for tampons?
Sheep.

So why do elephants have trunks?
Because sheep don't have strings.

* * *

Johnson went off on his annual hunting trip, bagged a pheasant, and proudly brought it home for dinner that night. After a few mouthfuls his wife jumped up and ran to the bathroom. Returning to the table, she whispered, "Honey, there were little black things in my shit. What could it be?"

"Just birdshot; guess I didn't clean the pheasant too well," explained Johnson. "But it won't hurt you."

A few minutes later his daughter dashed for the bathroom and came out crying. "Daddy, Daddy, there's little black things in my pee."

"Just birdshot, sweetie; I'm sorry. But don't worry, it won't hurt you."

Soon enough his son got up from the table, and came back ten minutes later looking rather strange. "What's wrong, Billy?" asked his dad nervously.

"I was jerking off and I shot the dog."

* * *

Did you hear about the alligators in Palm Beach sporting little WASPs on their T-shirts?

* * *

An elephant was walking along the jungle path when he got a thorn in his foot. He was unable to extract it, and had just about given up all hope when an ant came along. "Will you get this thorn out, please, ant?" pleaded the elephant.

"If I get to do what I want to do," piped the tiny insect in response.

"And what's that?" inquired the elephant.

"I want to fuck you in the ass."

Well, the elephant's foot was killing him by now, and besides, how bad could it be? So he agreed to the terms and the little bug set to work. In a few minutes the thorn was out. "Are you ready now?" squeaked the ant.

Being an honorable creature, the elephant replied that he was as ready as he'd ever be, and lay still while the ant made his way around the huge beast and began to fuck him in the ass.

A monkey had observed the entire transaction from up in a tree. Unable to contain himself any longer at the preposterous sight of the tiny insect pumping away at the elephant's rear, the monkey began chucking down coconuts, and succeeded in hitting the elephant right on the head.

"Ouch!" complained the elephant.

"Take it all, bitch!" cried the ant.

* * *

What's the difference between meat and fish?

If you beat your fish, it dies.

* * *

A young man was delighted to be asked home to meet the parents of a woman he was crazy about, and extremely eager to make a good impression. He was pretty nervous though, and by the time he arrived punctually at 6:30, his stomach was churning. The problem developed into one of acute flatulence, and halfway through cocktails, the young man realized he couldn't contain himself one second longer. A tiny fart escaped.

"Spot!" called out his girlfriend's mother to the family dog, who was lying at the visitor's feet.

Very relieved that the dog was getting blamed, the young man let go another, slightly larger one.

"Spot!" she called out sharply.

"I've got it made," thought the fellow to himself. One more and he'd be feeling fine. So he cut a really big one.

"*Spot!*" shrieked his hostess. "Get over here before he shits on you!"

* * *

A guy comes into a bar with a frog and sets it down next to the prettiest girl there. "This is a very special frog," he informs her. "His name is Charlie."

"What's so special about it?" she asks.

"He can eat pussy."

The girl slaps him so hard he falls off his chair, and calls him a disgusting liar. But no, he assures her, it's completely true. And after a couple of drinks and much discussion, she agrees to come back to his apartment to experience the frog in action. She positions herself on his bed, the guy places the frog between her legs, and says, "Okay, Charlie, do your stuff!"

To his owner's obvious embarrassment, the frog just sits there. In fact, no amount of coaxing and threatening gets the frog to move an inch. Finally, the guy sighs, picks up the frog, and says, "Okay, Charlie, but I'm only going to show you one more time."

* * *

A blind man walked into a department store with his seeing-eye dog and headed for the men's department. Surrounded by pajamas and neckties, he proceeded to come to a stop, pick up his German Shepherd by the hind legs, and swing the dog around in a circle.

A startled clerk ran over and asked loudly, "May I help you, sir?"

"No thanks," replied the blind man, "just looking."

* * *

Define *blind spot*.

What Dick and Jane do to be cruel.

* * *

This little kid is taking a walk with his father around the neighborhood, and what should they come across in an empty lot but two dogs going at it furiously. "Daddy," asks the kid, tugging at his father's sleeve, "what're those dogs doing?"

"They're making puppies, son."

A week later Billy gets thirsty in the middle of the night and wanders into his parents' bedroom. "Daddy, what're you and Mommy doing?" he asks plaintively.

"Well, Billy," says his slightly red-faced father, "we're making a baby."

"Roll her over, Daddy," cries the little boy, "I'd rather have puppies!"

* * *

A man was surprised by the sight of a farmer walking down the sidewalk with a three-legged pig on a leash. Unable to restrain his curiosity, he crossed the street and commented, "Quite a pig you have there."

"Let me tell you about this pig," offered its owner eagerly. "It's the most amazing animal in the world. Why, one night my house caught on fire when my wife and I were out, and this pig carried my three children to safety and put the fire out before the firemen could get there."

His listener whistled in admiration. "So why—"

"And that's not all," the farmer continued. "My house was broken into one night and this pig had the thief tied up and our valuables put back in place before my wife and I got to the bottom of the stairs."

"Pretty impressive," conceded the first man. "But how come—"

"And listen to this," interrupted the proud owner again. "When I fell through the ice on the pond last winter, this pig dove in and pulled me out. This pig saved my life!"

"That's fantastic. But I have to know one thing: How come the pig only has three legs?"

Shaking his head at his listener's stupidity, the farmer explained, "Hey, a pig like this you don't eat all at once."

* * *

"Now cheer up, Paul," soothed his buddy Bill over a couple of Budweisers. "You and Louise seem to be doing just fine. And it seems a little silly for you to be jealous of a German Shepherd, frankly. After all, you work all day and you live out in the sticks. That dog's good company for Louise."

"Good company!" snorted Paul, nearly spilling his beer. "Hey, the other night I caught her douching with Gravy Train."

* * *

The Easterner had always dreamed of owning his own cattle ranch, and finally made enough money to buy himself the spread of his dreams in Wyoming. "So what did you name the ranch?" asked his best friend when he flew out to visit.

"My wife and I had a hell of a time," admitted the new cowboy. "Couldn't agree on anything. We finally settled on the Double R Lazy L Triple Horseshoe Bar-7 Lucky Diamond Ranch."

"Wow." His friend was impressed. "So where are all the cows?"

"None of 'em survived the branding."

* * *

Why are dogs better than kids?

When you get tired of your dog, you can put it to sleep.

RELIGIOUS

What did the Zen master say to the hot dog vendor?

"Make me one with everything."

* * *

Did you hear about the kid whose father was Jewish and whose mother was Catholic?

Every time he went to confession he brought his lawyer along.

* * *

Old Mrs. Watkins awoke one spring morning to find that the river had flooded not only her basement but the whole first floor of her house. And, looking out her bedroom window, she saw that the water was still rising.

Two men in a passing rowboat shouted up an invitation to row to safety with them.

"No thank you," answered Mrs. Watkins tartly. "The Lord will provide." The men shrugged and rowed on.

By evening the water had risen so much that Mrs. Watkins was forced to climb out onto her roof, where she was spotted by a cheerful man in a motorboat. "Don't worry, lady," he yelled across the water, "I'll pick you right up."

"Please don't bother—the Lord will provide." And Mrs. Watkins turned her back on her would-be rescuer. "Suit yourself," he said, buzzing off.

Pretty soon Mrs. Watkins was forced to take refuge on her chimney, the only part of her house which was still above water. Fortunately a Red Cross cutter came by on patrol. "Jump in, lady," urged a rescue worker.

"No thank you," said Mrs. Watkins. "The Lord will provide."

So the boat went on, the water rose, and Mrs. Watkins drowned. Dripping wet and quite annoyed, she came through the Pearly Gates and demanded to see God. "What happened?" she demanded furiously. "I thought the Lord would *provide*."

"For cryin' out loud, lady," answered God wearily, "I sent *three boats*."

* * *

How do nuns play Religious Roulette?

They stand in a circle and blaspheme and see who gets struck by lightning first.

* * *

Jesus was making his usual rounds in Heaven when he noticed a wizened, white-haired old man sitting in a corner looking very disconsolate. The next week he was disturbed to come across him again, looking equally miserable, and a week later he stopped to talk to him.

"See here, old fellow," said Jesus kindly, "this is Heaven. The sun is shining, you've got all you need to eat and drink, clouds to recline on, harps to play—you should be blissfully happy! What's wrong?"

"Well," explained the old man, "you see, I was a carpenter on earth, and I lost my only, dearly beloved son at an early age. And here in Heaven I was hoping more than anything else to find him."

Tears sprang into Jesus's eyes. "Father!" he cried.

The old man jumped to his feet, burst into tears, and cried, "Pinocchio!"

* * *

What did the dyslexic rabbi say after a particularly rough day?

"Yo!"

* * *

The Pope is working on a crossword puzzle on Sunday afternoon. He stops for a moment or two, scratches his forehead, then asks the Cardinal, "Say, can you think of a four-letter word for 'woman' that ends in 'u-n-t?' "

"Aunt," replies the Cardinal.

"Say, thanks," says the Pope. "Got an eraser?"

* * *

Bumper sticker: Save Soviet Jewry—Win Valuable Prizes.

* * *

What do Catholic girls give each other at their bridal showers?

Vibrating crucifixes.

* * *

A Christian, a Moslem, and a Jew, all very pious, met at an interfaith congress and got to talking about the experiences that had inspired their religious devotion.

The Christian recounted being on a plane when it ran into a terrible storm over a remote wilderness area. "There was lightning and thunder all around us, and the pilot told us to brace for the crash. I dropped to my knees and prayed to God to save us—and then for one thousand feet all around us the wind calmed and the rain stopped. We made it to the airport, and since then my faith has never wavered."

The Moslem then told of a terrifying incident on his pilgrimage to Mecca. "A tremendous sandstorm came up out of nowhere, and within minutes my camel and I were almost buried. Sure I was going to die, I prostrated myself towards Mecca and prayed to Allah to deliver me. And suddenly, for one thousand feet all around me, the swirling dust settled and I was able to make my way safely across the desert. Since then I have been the devoutest of believers."

Nodding respectfully, the Jew then told his tale. "One Sabbath I was walking back from the temple when I saw a huge sack of money just lying there at the edge of the road. It had clearly been abandoned, and I felt it was mine to take, but obviously this would have been a violation of the Sabbath. So I dropped to my knees and prayed to Yahweh—and suddenly, for one thousand feet all around me, it was Tuesday."

* * *

Did you hear about the new Cabbage Patch Dolls for atheists' kids?

They're stuffed with catnip and dressed as early Christians.

* * *

When a live sex show opened up on Main Street, the town's clergymen formed a delegation to check out the show and determine its risk to their congregations. Coming out of the theater, they all agreed that it was truly a terrible show, with no redeeming value, miserable even as entertainment. Suddenly the Episcopal minister stopped. "I have to go back in—I forgot my hat."

"No you didn't," pointed out the priest. "It's hanging on your lap."

* * *

What did Jesus say while he was hanging on the cross?

"This is a hell of a way to spend Easter vacation."

* * *

When the Mother Superior answered the knock at the convent door, she found two leprechauns shuffling their feet on the doorsill. "Aye an' begorrah, Mother Superior," said the foremost one after an awkward pause, "would ye be havin' any leprechaun nuns in your church?"

The nun shook her head solemnly.

The little man shuffled his feet a bit more, then piped up, "An' would there be any leprechaun nuns in the convent?"

"No, my boys," said the Mother Superior gravely.

"Ye see, laddy," cried the leprechaun, whirling around to his companion triumphantly. "I *told* you ye been fuckin' a penguin!"

* * *

A rabbi, a priest, and a minister were discussing how they divided up the collection plate. The minister explained that he drew a circle on the ground and tossed the collection in the air. All the money that landed in the circle was God's, and all that landed outside the minister kept for himself and the parish.

The priest described a similar system: He drew a line on the ground, and everything that landed on the right side was for God and on the left for himself and the church.

The rabbi said that his system worked along somewhat the same lines. "I toss the collection up in the air," he explained, "and anything God can catch, He can keep."

* * *

What's the difference between Jesus Christ and an oil painting?

You only need one nail to hang up a painting.

* * *

Yitzhak Rabin invited the Pope to play a round of golf on his next visit to Jerusalem. Since the Pope had no idea how to play, he convened the College of Cardinals to ask their advice. "Call Jack Nicklaus," they suggested, "and let him play in your place. Tell Rabin you're sick or something."

Honored by His Holiness's request, Nicklaus agreed to represent him on the links. The Pope, again with advice from his staff, made him a cardinal just in case the Prime Minister were to get suspicious.

When Nicklaus returned from the match, the Pope asked him how he had done. "I came in second," was the reply.

"You mean to tell me Rabin beat you?" the pontiff screeched.

"No, Your Holiness," said Jack. "Rabbi Palmer did."

* * *

Did you hear about the dyslexic agnostic insomniac?

He lies awake all night wondering if there really is a dog.

* * *

Why did they send so many women with PMS to the Gulf War?

They fight like animals, and they retain water for four days.

* * *

Christ is on the cross and Peter is down the hill comforting Mary Magdalene when he hears a faint voice: "Peter . . . Peter . . . "

"I must go to my Savior," declared Peter, and headed steadfastly up the hill, only to be beaten and kicked back down the hill by the Roman centurions guarding the cross. But again he hears, even more faintly, "Peter . . . Peter . . . "

"He is in need, I must go." Peter limps back up the hill, leans a ladder up against the cross, and is halfway up to Jesus when the soldiers knock the ladder to the ground, beat him brutally, and send him rolling down the hill again.

Mary Magdalene is salving his wounds when he hears, "Peter . . . Peter . . . " this time barely audible. Peter crawls up the hill, drags himself up the ladder, and finally draws even with Christ's face just as the centurions are reaching for him.

"Peter . . . Peter . . . " says Jesus faintly, "I can see your house from here."

* * *

A little Catholic kid was praying as hard as he could. "God, I really, really want a car." Dashing to the window, he observed that the driveway was still empty.

"God," he prayed urgently, dropping to his knees again, "I really *need* a car." Still no result. Suddenly the kid jumped up again, ran into his parents' room, and grabbed the statuette of the Virgin Mary off the mantelpiece. He wrapped it up in ten layers of paper, using three rolls of tape and a spool of twine, then stuffed it inside a box at the very bottom of his closet.

"Okay, God," he said, getting back on his knees, "if you ever want to see your mother again . . . "

* * *

An ambitious new sales rep for Budweiser traveled all the way to Rome and managed to finagle an audience with the Pope himself. As soon as the two were alone together, he leaned over and whispered, "Your Holiness, I have an offer I think might interest you. I'm in a position to give you a million dollars if you'll change the wording in the Lord's Prayer to 'our daily beer.' Now whaddaya say?"

"Absolutely not," said the shocked Pontiff.

"Hey, I understand; it's a big decision," sympathized the salesman. "How about five million to make it easier?"

"I couldn't think of it," sputtered the Pope.

"I know it's a tough one. Tell you what—I can go up to fifty million dollars," proposed the salesman.

Asking him to leave the room, the Pope called in a Cardinal and whispered, "When does our contract with Pillsbury expire?"

* * *

Why don't Baptists screw standing up?

They're afraid it might lead to dancing.

* * *

One day God decided He was overdue for a vacation. "I hear Mars is nice," suggested St. Peter.

God shook His head. "I'm still sore from the sunburn I got there ten thousand years ago."

"I had a good time on Pluto," said the Archangel Gabriel.

"No way," said God. "I nearly broke my neck skiing there last millennium."

"There's always Earth," suggested a cherub meekly.

"Are you nuts?" yelled God. "I dropped by there two thousand years ago, and they're still sore at me for knocking up some Jewish chick."

* * *

Three nuns are waiting for an audience with Mother Theresa. The first goes in and says, "Forgive me, Mother, but I have seen a man's private parts."

"Go wash your eyes in holy water," instructs the aged nun.

The second nun confesses to Mother Theresa that she has touched a man's private parts. "My child," says the older woman, "go wash your hands in holy water."

The two nuns are busy washing themselves as penance when they're joined by the third nun. "Move over girls," she says. "I gotta gargle."

* * *

Thoroughly exasperated with her ornery seven-year-old, Mrs. McGuire finally said threateningly, "Marina, if you don't start behaving yourself, you'll never get to heaven."

"I don't want to go to heaven," replied the child promptly.

"Why on earth not?" asked her surprised mother.

"I'm afraid God might sneeze, and I wouldn't know what to say to him."

* * *

How many Zen Buddhists does it take to screw in a light bulb?

Two. One to screw it in and one to not screw it in.

How about Christian Scientists?

One—to pray for the light to go back on by itself.

* * *

One night little Johnny finished his prayers with "God bless Grandma," and the very next day his grandmother kicked the bucket. Johnny told his family about his prayer but no one seemed to give it too much thought. A week later he ended his prayers with, "God bless Grandpa," and the next day his grandfather died. The family was running a little scared by now, and when Johnny finished his prayers one night with, "God bless Daddy," his mother thought maybe she better warn her husband about it.

All that night Johnny's dad tossed and turned, and the next day he came home from work early. "I had a terrible day worrying about all this," he confided to his wife.

"You think you had a bad day," she blurted. "The mailman came to the door and dropped dead."

* * *

"Someone stole my bike," complained a priest to his minister friend.

"Bring up the ten commandments in your sermon tomorrow and as soon as you mention 'Thou shalt not steal' the guilty party will come forward," the minister confidently proposed.

The next day, the priest rode by the minister's house on his newly recovered bike. "I took your advice," he reported cheerfully, "and when I came to 'Thou shalt not commit adultery,' I remembered where I'd left it."

* * *

How did the repressed gay priest relieve his sexual tension?

He bought an inflatable bishop.

* * *

When the Eisenbergs moved to Italy, little Jaime came home from school in tears. He explained to his mother that the nuns were always asking these Catholic questions—and how was he, a nice Jewish boy, supposed to know the answers?

Mrs. Eisenberg's heart swelled with maternal sympathy and she determined to help her son out. "Jaime," she said, "I'm going to embroider the answers on the inside of your shirt and you just look down and read them the next time those nuns pick on you."

"Thanks, Mom," said Jaime, and he didn't bat an eye when Sister Michael asked him who the world's most famous virgin was. "Mary," he answered.

"Very good," said the nun. "And who was her husband?"

"Joseph," answered the boy.

"I see you've been studying. Now can you tell me the name of their son?"

"No problem," said Jaime. "Calvin Klein."

* * *

Heard about the new birth control pill for Catholic girls?

It weighs about six hundred pounds, and you roll it right in front of her bedroom door.

* * *

What's black and white and has a dirty name?

Sister Mary Fuckface.

* * *

A priest and a rabbi were out playing golf one day when the priest looked at his watch and said, "Pardon me, rabbi, but I must leave to go hear confession."

"What is this 'confession?'" asked the rabbi.

"It's when I listen to my parishioners tell me their sins and I absolve them while they say a penance," explained the priest.

"Interesting. Mind if I come along and watch?" asked the rabbi.

"Come on," said the priest, and they both crowded into the priest's side of the confessional.

The first penitent, a woman, came in and said, "Bless me Father, for I have sinned. I have had sex with a man three times."

"That's all right, my child," said the priest. "Put five dollars in the poor box and say three Hail Marys and you will be absolved."

In came a second woman. "Forgive me father, for I have sinned," she confessed. "I have had intercourse with a man three times."

"Don't worry about it," soothed the priest. "Put five dollars in the poor box, say five Hail Marys, and you will be absolved."

"Say, this looks easy," said the rabbi. "Mind if I give it a try?"

"Be my guest," said the priest as a third woman entered the confessional. "As long as they think it's me, they'll be forgiven."

"Forgive me father, for I have sinned," said the third penitent. "I have had sex with a man two times."

"Listen," said the rabbi, "go out and do it one more time. We're having a special today—three for five bucks."

* * *

Father Harris was motoring along a country lane in his parish on a spring afternoon when all of a sudden he got a flat tire. Exasperated, the priest stopped his car, got out and assessed the damage. Luckily, a four-wheel-drive jeep rounded the bend and pulled to a stop behind the crippled vehicle. The door to the jeep opened and out stepped a hulk of a man. "Good afternoon, Father," greeted the stranger. "Can I give you a hand?"

"Heaven be praised," rejoiced the priest. "As you can see, my son, I have a flat tire, and I must admit I've never changed one before."

"Don't worry about it, Father. I'll take care of it." And without skipping a beat, the bruiser picked up the front of the car with one hand and removed the lug nuts from the base of the flat tire with the other. "Why don't you get the spare from the trunk?" he asked.

"Why, ahh, yes, of course, my son," stuttered the amazed Father Harris. The priest rolled the spare around to the strongman, who casually lifted it up with his free hand, maneuvered it into place, and proceeded to tighten the lug nuts.

"Do you need any tools?" Father Harris asked.

His helper nodded. "These nuts are as tight as a nun's cunt."

"Hmmm," mused Father Harris. "I'd better get the wrench."

* * *

What's the worst thing about being an atheist?

You have no one to talk to when you're having an orgasm.

* * *

Seated next to an aged rabbi on a transcontinental flight, the eager young priest couldn't resist the opportunity to proselytize. "You really should think about coming over to the Roman Catholic faith and being welcomed into the arms of the Holy Father," he enthused earnestly. "Only those who believe in the Sacraments shall be admitted to the Kingdom of Heaven when they die, you know."

The rabbi nodded indulgently but expressed no interest in the mechanics of conversion, and eventually the young priest fell silent, depressed by his failure. Soon after, the plane ran into a tremendous hurricane, lost power, and crashed into the Illinois countryside. Miraculously the priest was thrown, unhurt, from his seat. When he came to and looked back at the flaming wreckage, the first thing he saw was the rabbi, crossing himself.

Crossing himself and whispering a brief prayer of gratitude, the priest ran over and took his arm. "Praise the Lord!" he babbled joyfully, "You *did* hear the Word after all, didn't you? And just in time for it to comfort you through mortal peril. And you do wish to be saved, to become one of us now. Alleluia!"

"Vat on earth are you talking about?" asked the elderly fellow, still rather dazed.

"Sir, I saw it with my own eyes. As you stepped out of the flames, you made the sign of the cross!"

"Cross? Vat cross?" asked the rabbi irritably. "I vas simply checking: spectacles, testicles, vallet and vatch."

* * *

Three guys die and are transported to the Pearly Gates, where St. Peter greets them warmly, explaining that there's just one brief formality before they can be admitted to Heaven. Each will have to answer a quick question. Turning to the first man, he asks, "What, please, is Easter?"

"That's an easy one. It's to celebrate when the Pilgrims landed. You buy a turkey and really stuff yourself—"

"You're out," interrupts St. Peter brusquely, turning to the second man. "What can you tell me about Easter?"

"No problem," he begins confidently. "It celebrates Jesus's birthday, and you go buy a tree and all these presents—"

"Forget it," says the saint. He looks at the third man. "I don't suppose you'd know anything about Easter?"

"Easter commemorates the day Jesus rises from the dead and comes to the mouth of the cave—"

"Go on, go on," interrupts an excited St. Peter.

"—and if he sees his shadow, there's going to be six more weeks of winter."

* * *

What do you get when you cross an agnostic with a Jehovah's Witness?

Someone who rings your doorbell on Sunday morning for no particular reason.

* * *

Jesus and Moses went golfing, and were about even until they reached the fifteenth hole, a par five. Both balls landed about twenty feet from the edge of a little pond that stood between them and the hole. Moses took out a 5-wood and landed his ball in excellent position. Jesus took out a 5-iron.

"Hang on, hang on," cautioned Moses. "Use a wood—you'll never make it."

"If Arnold Palmer can make that shot with a 5-iron, so can I," said Jesus. His ball landed in the middle of the lake. Moses parted the waters, retrieved the ball, and sighed when he saw Jesus still holding the 5-iron.

"If Arnold Palmer can make that shot with a 5-iron, so can I," maintained Jesus. Again Moses had to part the waters to retrieve the ball. By this time there were a number of people waiting to play through, and Moses said firmly, "Listen, Jesus, I'm not fetching the ball another time. Use a wood." Jesus, however, still insisted, "If Arnold Palmer can make that shot with a 5-iron, so can I." Splash! Moses shook his head. "I told you, I'm not budging. Get it yourself." So Jesus walked off across the water towards where the ball had landed.

At this, the onlookers gaped in astonishment. One came over to Moses and stammered, "I can't believe my eyes—that guy must think he's Jesus Christ!"

Moses shook his head gloomily. "He *is* Jesus Christ. He *thinks* he's Arnold Palmer."

CELEBRITIES

Why do the Clintons take Chelsea everywhere?
    So they won't have to kiss her good-bye.

* * *

Why did Arnold Schwarzenegger and Maria Shriver marry?
    They want to breed the first bulletproof Kennedy.

* * *

Did you hear about the Colonel Khaddafi doll?
    Wind it up and it takes Barbie and Ken hostage.

How about the Richard Simmons doll?
    Wind it up and it ignores Barbie and asks Ken out for a drink.

* * *

What did Dan Quayle say when they asked him to spell Mississippi?
    "The state or the river?"

* * *

When the brash young advertising executive arrived at La Coupole for his lunch appointment, he spotted Rupert Murdoch at a corner table and went right over. "Excuse me for interrupting your meal, Mr. Murdoch," he began, "but I know how much you appreciate enterprise and initiative. I'm trying to win over a very important account today—it could really make or break my company—and the clients I'm meeting with would be incredibly impressed if you stopped by our table at some point and said, 'Hello, Mike.' It would be an incredible favor Mr. Murdoch, and some day I'd make it up to you."

    "Okay, okay," sighed Murdoch, and went back to his smoked

pheasant. He finished and was putting on his coat when he remembered the young man's request. Obligingly he went over to his table, tapped him on the shoulder, and said, "Hi, Mike."

"Not now, Rupert," snapped the young man. "Can't you see I'm eating?"

* * *

What's blond, has big boobs, and lives in Sweden?
Salman Rushdie.

* * *

Have you seen Salman Rushdie's new book?
It's called *Buddha, the Fat Fuck*.

* * *

What's black and crispy and comes on a stick?
Joan of Arc.

* * *

Why did God invent liquor?
So a Kennedy wouldn't be Pope.

* * *

How does Linda Lovelace masturbate?
(Clear your throat.)

* * *

What did Karen Carpenter say when she saw the witch melt away in "The Wizard of Oz"?
"Now, *that's* a diet!"

* * *

What do Winnie the Pooh and John the Baptist have in common?
The same middle name.

* * *

When you have Jerry Brown, Bill Clinton, and Jane Fonda together in a room, who stands out?
Jane Fonda—because she's actually been to Vietnam.

* * *

Queen Elizabeth and Lady Di are out for a drive in the Bentley one Sunday afternoon, and slow down for a man signalling for help from the roadside. But no sooner has the car come to a stop than he springs to the door, and pulls out a gun. "Hand over that fancy diamond tiara you wear in all the postcards," he snarls to the queen.

"I'm terribly sorry to disappoint you, my good man," responds the queen, "but I never wear my tiara on Sundays."

"Shit." The robber turns to Diana. "Okay, cough up that fancy engagement ring."

"I'm terribly sorry," says Lady Di sweetly, "but I'm afraid I didn't put it on this morning. It must be on my night table back at the palace."

"Aw, hell," growls the robber, "I'll have to settle for the car." The queen and the princess get out, and off he drives, leaving the two women by the road. After a few minutes have passed, Diana asks, "Pardon me, Your Highness, but didn't you have that tiara on when we set out this morning?"

"Indeed I did," replies the queen, blushing ever so slightly and pointing delicately downwards. "I hid it . . . down there. And I'm quite certain you had your engagement ring on, now didn't you?"

Blushing, Diana nodded, and confessed to having resorted to the same hiding place. They start down the road towards London when Queen Elizabeth lets out a little sigh. "I do wish Princess Margaret had been with us," she explains. "We could have saved the Bentley."

* * *

What do Yoko Ono and the Ethiopians have in common?
Living off dead beetles.

* * *

How many times does 59 go into 21?
I dunno—ask Woody Allen.

* * *

Did you hear about Woody Allen's new TV show?
It's called "Make Room for Daddy."

His new movie?
"Honey, I Fucked the Kids."

* * *

Not long after David Dinkins was elected Mayor of New York, he was riding home with his wife in the limousine. And who should they spot on a street corner but a man, none too prosperous looking, to whom Mrs. Dinkins had once been engaged.

Dinkins turned to her and said smugly, "Now aren't you glad you married *me*?"

"If I'd married *him*," she responded tartly, "*he'd* be mayor."

* * *

Who are N, O, and P?

    Mary Beth Whitehead's next three kids.

* * *

Why did Snow White divorce the Prince?

    Turns out he couldn't get it up unless she was unconscious.

* * *

What do you get when you cross a great painter with a really rude person?

    Vincent Van Go Fuck Yourself.

* * *

Why did Dolly Parton's teeth fall out?

    Her dentist couldn't reach them.

* * *

Why couldn't Lois Lane get an abortion?

    The fetus kept bending the doctor's tools.

* * *

What was Humpty Dumpty's last thought?

    "Oh my God, I'm not wearing clean underwear!"

* * *

What'll it take to reunite the Beatles?

    Three more bullets.

* * *

What do you do when you have Saddam Hussein, Muammar Khaddafi, and Al Sharpton in one room but you only have two bullets?

    Shoot Sharpton twice, to make sure he's dead.

* * *

What was Ted Kennedy's advice to Clarence Thomas when he was accused by Anita Hill of sexual harassment?

    "Why didn't you just drown the bitch?"

What was Thomas's response?

    "At least they're alive when I'm done with them."

* * *

How come Roseanne Arnold never goes to the beach?

    Because members of Greenpeace keep pushing her back in the water.

* * *

Why can't you get Pee Wee Herman's agent on the phone?

    These days he's handling himself.

* * *

What's this? (Make a loose fist.)
Pee Wee's playhouse.

* * *

What does Wisconsin produce more of than any other state?
Cannibals!

* * *

Did you know Jeffrey Dahmer's apartment is for rent?
It comes with a roommate—but some assembly is required.

* * *

Batman and Superman were assigned to a crime-watch patrol one day, and Batman noticed that Superman's clothes were torn and his face bruised. When he asked what had happened, Superman explained that he'd been flying home when he'd spotted Catwoman sunbathing nude on her rooftop. "I didn't want to give her a chance to run for her clothes, so I snuck up from behind and jumped on top of her."
"Was she surprised?" asked Batman.
"Not half as surprised as the Invisible Man."

* * *

What did Madonna say to King Kong?
"Is it in yet?"

* * *

Why does Madonna's diet consist mainly of salads?
She eats like a rabbit, too.

* * *

How can you spot Dolly Parton's kids in the playground?
Stretch marks around their lips.

* * *

What kind of wood doesn't float?
Natalie.

* * *

Why didn't Natalie shower on the boat?
She preferred to wash up on shore.

* * *

What did the seven dwarfs say when the prince woke Snow White?
"Guess it's back to jerking off."

* * *

Why haven't they cremated Colonel Sanders yet?

They can't decide whether to do him regular or crispy.

* * *

What do you get when you cross a Cabbage Patch Doll with the Pillsbury Doughboy?

A bitch with a yeast infection.

* * *

"How do you feel about having been born blind?" asked a sympathetic reporter of Stevie Wonder.

"It could've been worse," answered the singer philosophically. "I could've been born black!"

* * *

Entering his prison cell for the first time, child-murderer Joel Steinberg was introduced to his cellmate, a six-foot-four inch black serving twenty-five years for rape and manslaughter. "We gonna to be in here for a long, long time," commented the cellmate.

With a nervous nod, Steinberg acknowledged that this was so.

"Such a long time that it's kinda like a marriage, wouldn't ya say?"

"Sure," conceded Steinberg.

"And in every marriage there's a husband and a wife, right?" the giant black guy continued relentlessly.

"Right," Steinberg admitted, breaking into a cold sweat.

"So what yo wanna be, de husband or de wife?"

"The husband," blurted Steinberg with a sigh of relief.

"Fine," commented his roommate, settling his huge frame on the bottom bunk bed. "Now get ovah heah and suck yo' wife's dick."

* * *

Why was David Kennedy buried at sea?

So Uncle Ted could drive to the funeral.

* * *

What's yellow and sleeps alone?

Yoko Ono.

* * *

As JFK lay dying in a Dallas Hospital, he called feebly for his brother Teddy, who was pacing outside. Rushing in, Teddy cradled his dying brother in his arms as he tried to make out the President's last garbled words. "I can't hear you, Jack," he cried, tears running down his face.

In one last effort, the valiant statesman pulled his brother's head close and uttered the precious words: "Mary Jo puts out."

* * *

What do Alex Haley and Suzanne Somers have in common?

Black roots.

* * *

What's the worst thing about massacring a thousand Chinese students?

An hour later, you feel like massacring a thousand more.

* * *

Why did Karen Carpenter shoot her dog?

It kept trying to bury her.

* * *

The attractive woman turned to the man in the business suit behind her in the elevator. "Excuse me," she asked, "but are you Donald Trump?"

The man cleared his throat. "Yes, as a matter of fact, I am."

"Oh," she gushed, "I've *always* wanted to meet you, Mr. Trump. And now that we're together," she continued throatily, "I'll tell you what I'd like to do: I'm inviting you back to my room, where I'll kneel in front of you and pull out your cock and suck it till it's harder than it's ever been before, and suck it some more until you come all over my face . . . "

"Hang on a sec," interrupted Trump. "What's in it for me?"

* * *

Did you hear Jimmy Swaggart's starting up a new magazine?

It's called *Repenthouse*.

* * *

How do Ted Bundy's friends commemorate his death?

They lay a wreath on the fuse box.

OLD AGE

What're the good things about having Alzheimer's?

You're always meeting new people, and you can hide your own Easter eggs.

* * *

Brent woke up in the middle of the night and cried until his mother came in to see what was the matter. "I have to make pee-pee," wailed the little boy.

"All right," said his mother, "I'll take you to the bathroom."

"No," insisted Brent, "I want Grandma."

"Don't be silly, I can do the same thing as Grandma," said his mother firmly.

"Huh-uh. Her hands shake."

* * *

What's 10, 9, 8, 7, 6, 5, 4, 3, 2, 1?

Bo Derek getting older.

* * *

Three old guys were debating whose ailments and afflictions were the worst. "Have I got a problem?" the seventy-year-old complained. "Every morning I get up at seven-thirty and have to take a piss, but then I have to stand at the toilet for half an hour because my pee barely trickles out."

"Heck, that's nothing," maintained the eighty-year-old. "Every morning at eight-thirty I have to take a dump, but I'm so constipated I have to sit on the can for an hour and a half. It's terrible."

The ninety-year-old moaned, "And you guys think you have it rough? Every morning at seven-thirty I piss like a racehorse, and at eight-thirty I shit like a pig."

"So what's the problem?" asked his buddies indignantly.

"I don't wake up till ten."

* * *

The aged couple came into town for their annual physical. "You go in first, Paw," said the old woman, settling down to her knitting in the waiting room.

In a little while, the old codger stuck his head out of the doctor's office. "Maw," he called out, scratching his head, "do we have intercourse?"

"If I've told you once, I've told you a dozen times, Paw," she scolded, "we have Blue Cross and Blue Shield."

* * *

The old couple sat through the porno movie twice, not getting up to leave until the theater was closing for the night. "You folks must have really enjoyed the show," commented the usher on the way out.

"It was revolting," retorted the old lady.

"Disgusting," added her husband.

"Then why did you sit through it twice?" asked the puzzled usher.

"We had to wait until you turned up the house lights," explained the old woman. "We couldn't find my underpants, and his teeth were in them."

* * *

What do old women have between their tits that young women don't?

A belly button.

* * *

A dutiful son, Andrew accompanied his dad to his regular check-ups with the urologist. "And how's your urine flow, Mr. Gunderson?" asked the doctor once they were seated in his office.

"Fine, just fine, Doctor, and God helps," quavered Gunderson cheerfully. "He turns the light on when I start, turns it off when I stop, and I don't have to do a thing."

"Oh no," groaned the son as the puzzled urologist looked over at him. "Dad's peeing in the refrigerator again."

* * *

Did you hear about the aging movie star?

If she has her face lifted again, she'll be a bearded lady.

* * *

The seventy-seven-year-old tycoon and his twenty-six-year-old bride were on their way from the wedding reception to the honeymoon suite at the Plaza when he had a tremendous heart attack. Paramedics labored furiously over his frail body as the ambulance rushed across town.

The millionaire's pulse remained feeble and erratic, and one of the medics turned to the young bride. "How about giving your husband a few words of encouragement, Mrs. Dillon? I think he could use them," he suggested.

"Okay," she agreed with a shrug, leaning towards the stretcher. "Bill, honey, I hope you perk up real fast. I'm so horny I'm ready to hump one of these cute guys in white."

* * *

How did the supermarket double its pet-food sales in one week?

Instituted a senior-citizens discount.

So why did the old lady starve to death?

She was mugged by a Doberman on the way home.

* * *

One night twelve-year-old Ollie and his grandfather slept in the same bed so they could get an early start on their fishing trip the next morning. In the middle of the night, the old man elbowed the boy in the ribs and whispered urgently, "Go get Grandma, quick, and bring her in here—you get back to your own room."

"Forget it, Grandpa," said the boy. "That's my dick you're holding."

* * *

How do you know when you're really old?

You can remember championship fights between two white guys.

* * *

Hector had always been quite the ladies' man, but as he moved into his later years he was increasingly demoralized by his waning sexual prowess. One night as he was walking back to his apartment he saw a frog in the middle of the sidewalk. "If you pick me up and kiss me," propositioned the frog, "I'll turn into a gorgeous woman."

Hector leaned over and popped the frog in his breast pocket.

"Hey," complained the frog, "aren't you gonna kiss me? I'll turn into the woman of your dreams, and you can have your way with me as much as you want, I promise."

"Thanks, anyway," replied the old man with a shrug. "At my age, I'd rather have a talking frog."

* * *

Carla was well into her sixties when she went to her doctor complaining of nausea, exhaustion, and occasional cramps. After a thorough examination the doctor sent her to the hospital for a battery of tests, and finally confronted her with the results. "Mrs. Barber, medically impossible though it seems at your age, there's no doubt about it: you're pregnant."

"Impossible," she cried, and fainted dead away. When she came to, she staggered to the phone, dialed her seventy-eight-year-old husband, and screeched, "You've knocked me up, you randy old goat!"

There was a long pause at the other end of the line. Then a voice said, "And to whom am I speaking?"

* * *

How can you tell when your wife's getting old?

You can suck her tit and go down on her just by turning your head.

* * *

Two old guys used to meet in the park on sunny afternoons and talk baseball. As they got older and more frail, their thoughts turned to the afterlife and they got to wondering whether there would be baseball in Heaven. So they promised each other that whoever passed away first would somehow let the other know.

Eddie was the first to die. A week after his funeral, his buddy was woken by a voice from outside his window, Joe's voice. "Eddie, listen up," it said. "I've got some good news and some bad news. The good news is that there's baseball up here."

"And the bad news?" quavered Joe.

"The bad news is that you're pitching on Friday."

* * *

What's the difference between an old man and a penis?

When you hold a penis, the wrinkles disappear.

* * *

144

Just as the elderly woman was turning her Mercedes into a parking space at the mall, she was edged out by a red Firebird. "You've got to be young and fast," jeered the teenaged driver as he jumped out from behind the wheel.

The woman reversed, revved her engine, and rammed the Firebird. As the Mercedes reversed and headed for his car again, the teenager turned and gaped, then ran over and banged on the woman's window. "What the hell do you think you're doing?" he screeched.

She smiled sweetly. "You've got to be old and rich."

* * *

The girls in the whorehouse were frankly skeptical when a ninety-year-old man came in and put his money down on the front desk, but finally a good-hearted hooker took him up to her room. Imagine her surprise when he proceeded to make love to her with more energy and skill than any man she had ever known. "I've never come so many times," she gasped. "How about once more, on the house?"

"All right," conceded the old geezer, "but I have to take a five-minute nap and you must keep your hands on my penis, just so, while I'm asleep." She agreed eagerly, and as soon as he woke up he gave her an even better lesson in lovemaking.

"Oh God," gasped the hooker ecstatically, "I can't get enough of you. Please, just once more—I'll pay *you*."

The old man agreed, subject to the same conditions. Just before he nodded out the hooker said, "Excuse me, but would you mind explaining about the nap and why I have to keep my hands on your privates?"

"I'm ninety years old," retorts the man, "so is it so surprising I need a little rest? As for the other, it's because the last time while I was napping they took my wallet."

* * *

An eager-beaver young real-estate agent was doing his best to sell this old coot a condominium in Palm Beach. Having outlined its many attractions in detail, he confidently concluded his pitch: "And, Mr. Rosenblatt, this is an investment in the future."

"Sonny," croaked Rosenblatt, "at my age I don't even buy green bananas."

* * *

At his annual checkup Bernie was given an excellent bill of health. "It must run in your family," commented the doctor. "How old was your dad when he died?"

"What makes you think he's dead?" asked Bernie. "He's eighty-six and going strong."

"Aha! And how long did your grandfather live?"

"What makes you think he's dead, doc? He's one hundred and ten years old and getting married to a twenty-two year old in two weeks," retorted Bernie.

"At his age!" exclaimed the doc. "Why's he want to marry a twenty-two-year-old?"

"Doc," said Bernie, "what makes you think he *wants* to?"

* * *

A teenager was riding in an elevator with a very old woman when a horrible smell filled the car. Finally the kid said, "Excuse me for asking, lady, but did you fart?"

"Of course I did, sonny," she replied sharply. "Think I always smell like that?"

* * *

The newlyweds came back from their honeymoon at Niagara Falls and moved into the apartment upstairs from the groom's parents, Vito and Nina. That night Vito was awakened by a dig in the ribs from his wife. "Vito, listen," she whispered. Sure enough, they could hear the bedsprings in the room above them creaking rhythmically. "Come on, Vito," she urged. So he rolled over on top of her and they made love.

He had just fallen back asleep when the creaking of the bedsprings woke him again. "Vito, listen to them," said Nina in a stage whisper. "Come *on*." So he rolled over and made love to her again.

Vito was sound asleep when another dig in the ribs woke him to the sound of the bedsprings creaking away yet another time. "Vito, *listen,*" began his wife, pulling off her nightgown.

At this the old man leapt to his feet, grabbed a broom, and started banging away on the ceiling like a maniac. "Cut it out, goddammit!" he yelled. "You're killing your old man!"

* * *

Sam wasn't happy about putting his dad in the state nursing home but it was all he could afford—until a lucky investment paid off.

The first thing he did with his new-found wealth was to move his father to the best nursing home available.

The old man was astounded by the luxury of his new surroundings. On the first day, he started to list to his right side in front of the television. Instantly a nurse ran over and tactfully straightened him out. Over lunch he started to lean a bit to the left, but within a few seconds a nurse gently pushed him upright again.

That night his son called. "How're you doing, Pop?" he asked eagerly.

"Oh Sam, it's a wonderful place," said the father. "I've got my own color TV, the food is cooked by a French chef, the gardens look like Versailles, you wouldn't believe."

"Dad, it sounds perfect."

"There's one problem with the place, though, Sammy," the father whispered. "They won't let you fart."

* * *

What's an optimist?

An octogenarian who's getting married and starts looking for a house in a good school district.

* * *

A woman was walking towards the bus stop when she came across a little old man sitting on the curb, sobbing his heart out. Moved by his grief, the woman bent over and asked him what was so terribly wrong.

"Well, you see," choked the old man, "I used to be married to this awful bitch. She was fat and ugly, never put out, the house was a pigsty, and she spent my money like water. She wasn't even a decent cook. My life was a horror."

The woman clucked sympathetically.

"After thirty years of living hell, she died," the old man went on with a sob, "and I met this beautiful woman. Thirty-eight years old, a body like Sophia Loren and face like an angel, a fabulous cook and housekeeper, the hottest thing in bed you could possibly imagine, and—can you believe it at my age?—crazy over me! She couldn't wait to marry me, and treats me like a prince in my own home."

"This doesn't sound so bad," volunteered the woman, frankly puzzled.

"I tell you, I'm the luckiest man in the world." The old coot bent over in a racking spasm, convulsed with sorrow.

"Well, then," she asked tentatively, "what's to be so unhappy about? Why are you crying on the street corner?"

"Because," he sobbed, "I can't remember where I live!"

* * *

"Doctor, I'm losing my sex urge," complained Ruth at her annual checkup.

"Mrs. Beeston, that's understandable at eighty-four," said the doctor, "but tell me: When did you first start noticing this?"

"Last night," she answered, "and then again this morning."

"Aha," said the doctor. "Your problem isn't a diminished sex drive, it's that you're not getting enough. You should be having sex at least fifteen times a month."

Thanking him and heading home, the old woman couldn't wait to report the doctor's prescription to her husband. "Guess what, Pop? He says I need it fifteen times a month!"

Pop put in his teeth and said, "That's just great, honey. Put me down for five."

* * *

Herschel was astounded—and a little worried—when Reuben announced his upcoming marriage to a twenty-year-old girl. "At your advanced age," cautioned his friend, "couldn't that be fatal?"

Reuben shrugged philosophically. "If she dies, she dies."

* * *

Talking to his friends on the front porch, ninety-two-year-old Ed reported, "I've got my health, my heart is strong, my liver is good, and my mind, knock wood . . . who's there?"

* * *

When old Mr. O'Leary died, an elaborate wake was planned. In preparation, Mrs. O'Leary called the undertaker aside for a private little talk. "Please be sure to attach his toupee to his head very securely. No one but I knew he was bald," she confided, "and he'd never rest in peace if anyone found out now. But our friends from the old country are sure to hold his hands and touch his head before they're through paying their last respects."

"Rest assured, Mrs. O'Leary," comforted the undertaker. "I'll fix it so that toupee will never come off."

•

Sure enough, the day of the wake the old timers gave O'Leary's ancient corpse quite a going-over, but the toupee never budged. At the end of the day, a delighted Mrs. O'Leary offered the undertaker five hundred dollars for handling the matter so professionally.

"Oh, I couldn't possibly accept your money," protested the undertaker. "What's a few nails?"

* * *

The retired couple was sitting at the table after their Sunday lunch when the wife looked over and said, "Know what I feel like? An ice cream. Will you go get me one?"

"Okay, honey," said the long-suffering husband, getting up.

"But not just any ice cream," she interrupted. "A sundae."

"Okay, dear, a sundae it is."

"But not just any sundae, a banana split. Should I write it down and put the note in your coat pocket?"

"No, dear," said the husband, pulling on his coat. "You want a special sundae, a banana split."

"Right, but not just any banana split. I want a scoop of chocolate on one side and a scoop of pistachio on the other. Sure you don't want me to write it down?"

"I got it, I got it," said the beleaguered husband, heading for the door.

"But that's not all," she shouted after him. "I want it to be special. I want whipped cream and a cherry on top. Let me write it down for you."

"No, no, no," protested her husband. "You want a special ice cream sundae: a banana split with a scoop of pistachio here, a scoop of chocolate there, some whipped cream, and a cherry on top."

"And don't forget the chopped nuts."

"Chopped nuts," repeated the husband as the door closed after him.

Two hours later the husband returned and put a greasy paper bag on the kitchen table. The wife walked over, looked inside, and saw four bagels. Looking up at him in intense irritation, she snarled, "I *knew* you'd forget the cream cheese."

* * *

Mrs. Garwood lived up in the hills and had always been healthy as a horse, but as old age approached, she found herself suffering from some "female troubles." Finally she confessed this to her daughter-in-law, who made an appointment with a gynecologist in the city and drove her in.

A wide-eyed Mrs. Garwood lay silent and still as a stone while the doctor examined her. When it was over, she sat up and fixed a beady eye on the physician. "You seem like such a nice young man," she quavered. "Tell me, does your mother know what you do for a living?"

* * *

A wealthy old gentleman desired the services of a prostitute, so he arranged for a call-girl service to send over their one-thousand-dollar, top-of-the-line girl. She got all dolled up and went up to his swank penthouse, where the door was opened by the elderly millionaire himself. "And what can I do for you tonight?" she asked in her throatiest voice, dropping her fur coat to reveal a spectacular body barely covered by a skimpy silk dress.

"Hot tub," he said.

So they went into his luxuriously appointed bathroom, where she settled him into the huge tub. "And now, sir?" she asked, bending over to show her cleavage to best advantage.

"Waves," he instructed.

So she kicked off her heels, perched on the edge of the tub, and proceeded to kick her feet vigorously in the water. "Next?"

"Thunder."

Obligingly banging her hand against the side of the tub, she gently reminded him that her special services were costly and that surely there was some sort of treat she could offer him . . . ?

He nodded. "Lightning."

Kicking her feet in the water, banging on the tub with one hand, and flicking the lights on and off with the other, she felt obliged to give it one more shot. "Sir, you know that sexual services are my specialty. Isn't there something along those lines you'd be interested in?"

"Are you crazy?" he retorted, looking up from the tub. "In *this* weather?"

MISCELLANEOUS

How do you make a dead baby float?
Two scoops of ice cream and a scoop of dead baby.

* * *

How did the dead baby cross the road?
Stapled to the chicken.

* * *

What's the perfect gift for a dead baby?
A dead puppy.

* * *

Two women were comparing notes on their psychotherapists. "Frankly, mine drives me crazy," said Eileen. "Two years I've been going to her now and she never says a single word to me. Just sits there and nods."

"That's nothing," responded Ruthie. "After six years I finally get three words out of mine."

"Oh yeah? What'd he say?"

" 'No hablo Ingles.' "

* * *

John's divorce left him lonely and horny, but after so many years away from the dating scene he was a little awkward about how to proceed. Still, with his doctor's encouragement, he did start to go out on a regular basis.

One Saturday night the doctor's phone rang. "I'm sorry to bother you at home," blurted John, obviously rather agitated, "but I just *had* to have your advice right away. See, I've met this terrific woman, we get along great, I really think she could be the one for me, everything's going great—"

"So?" interrupted the doctor, trying to conceal his irritation at having been summoned away from the dinner table.

"There's one little problem," John explained. "I really want to take her home with me, but I can't remember from our first date whether she said she had V.D. or T.B. What should I do?"

The doctor thought for a moment, then advised, "If she coughs, fuck her."

* * *

"I'm terribly worried about my son," confessed Mrs. Applegate to a psychiatrist a friend had recommended. "I came home early one day and caught him in the rec room with little four-year-old Emily from next door . . . and they both had their pants down."

"This sort of curiosity is very natural, Mrs. Applegate," the psychiatrist reassured her. "Try not to worry."

"I just can't help it," she said with a sniff. "And it's got my son's wife all upset, too."

* * *

The weary young mother collapsed on the bench at the bus stop, but the minute the stroller stopped moving, a howl came up from its little passenger. The young woman turned to the pleasant-looking matron sitting next to her. "Rachel cries day and night, every day. I can't get her to be quiet unless I'm pushing her in the stroller." She started to dry quietly. "I don't know how much longer I can keep this up . . . I'm getting desperate."

The older woman patted her arm soothingly. "Now, now, I know just how you feel. My William was just like that when I first brought him home. Lord, how he screamed."

"You mean you got him to quiet down?" The young mother's face lit up. "How? Please tell me."

"Of course I'll tell you, dear: the secret's a bottle with eight ounces of vodka and four Sominex ground up in it. Warm it so the tablets dissolve, you hear?"

That sounded rather drastic to the new mother, but she thanked her new acquaintance and went wearily on her way. And a few sleepless nights later, as her daughter screamed into the wee hours, she gave the home remedy a try.

A little while later the older woman was waiting at the same bus stop when she was accosted by the young mother, clearly distraught. "I can't believe you told me to give Rachel vodka and sleeping pills—it killed my baby!"

The woman replied calmly, "Mine too."

* * *

The careworn man decided to take a break and consult a fortune-teller during his lunch hour. She gathered her shawl around her, gazed deeply into her crystal ball, and solemnly intoned, "I see . . . I see a buried treasure . . . "

"I know, I know," her customer interrupted wearily, "my wife's first husband."

* * *

At her annual checkup, the attractive young woman was informed that it was necessary to have her temperature taken rectally. She agreed, but a few moments later cried indignantly, "Doctor, that's not my rectum!"

"And it's not my thermometer either," admitted the doctor with a grin.

Just then the woman's husband, who had come to pick her up, walked into the examining room. "What the hell's going on here?" he demanded.

"Just taking your wife's temperature," the doctor explained coolly.

"Okay, doc," grumbled the fellow, "but that thing better have numbers on it."

* * *

What were the most erotic words ever spoken on television?

"Gee, Ward, you were kind of rough on the Beaver last night."

* * *

One day Bobby's teacher tells the class they're going to play a thinking game, and asks for a volunteer. "Pick me, pick me," begs Bobby.

"Okay, Bobby," says the teacher. "Now I'm going to describe objects to you and you tell me what they are. Here we go: What's red, shiny, and you eat it?"

"A cherry," says Bobby.

"No, it's an apple, but it shows you're thinking," said the teacher gently. "Ready for the next one? What's yellow and you eat it?"

"A lemon," says Bobby.

"No," says the teacher, "it's a banana, but it shows you're thinking."

Before the teacher can continue, Bobby interrupts. "Okay, teacher, I've got one for you." He reaches into his pocket, looks down, pulls his hand out, and asks, "What's long, pink, and has a little red head on the end of it?"

"Oooh, Bobby!" squeals the teacher.

"No, it's a match—but it shows you're thinking."

* * *

As soon as they had finished making love, Susie jumped up from the bed and started packing her suitcase.

"What on earth are you doing?" asked her puzzled husband.

"In Las Vegas I could get two hundred dollars for what I just gave you for free," she pointed out, "so I'm moving to Las Vegas."

This was enough to provoke her husband to jump up and begin packing *his* bags.

"What're you up to?" asked Susie in surprise.

"I'm following you to Las Vegas," he replied. "I've *got* to see you live off six hundred dollars a year."

* * *

How many lawyers does it take to change a light bulb?

How many can you afford?

* * *

How many doctors does it take?

Does the bulb have insurance?

* * *

How many mothers does it take?

None—they don't make diapers that small.

* * *

How many Country & Western singers?

Two. One to change the bulb and the other to sing about all the good times she had with the old bulb.

* * *

How many convenience store clerks?

Who are you kidding? They won't even give you change for a dollar.

* * *

How many perverts?

None. Perverts don't screw light bulbs, they screw little children.

* * *

How many serial killers?

Just one. But first he has to dismember the old one and masturbate in front of it.

* * *

How many Mafiosi?

Three. One to change the bulb, one to be a witness, and the third to shoot the witness.

* * *

How many Japanese businessmen?

Six. One to screw it in and the others to come up with a plan for dumping the old one on the American market.

* * *

How many nuclear engineers?

Five. One to install the new one and four to debate what to do with the old one for the next millennium.

* * *

How many antiabortionists?

Four. One to change the bulb and three to swear that it was lit from the minute it touched the socket.

* * *

The homeowner got into his grubbiest clothes one Saturday morning and set about all the chores he'd been putting off for weeks. He'd cleaned out the garage, pruned the hedge, and was halfway through mowing the lawn when a guy pulled up in front of the house in a fancy sports car and called out, "Say, buddy, what do you get for that yard work?"

The fellow thought for a minute, then yelled back, "The lady who lives here lets me sleep with her."

* * *

Did you know that once you get married, you can look forward to three different kinds of sex?

—First there's House Sex, when you make love all over the house: on the floor, on the kitchen table, in the garage, anywhere, anytime.

—Then comes Bedroom Sex: every so often, once the kids are bathed and fed and asleep, the shades pulled, and the door locked, you make love in the bedroom.

—Last comes Hall Sex. That's when you pass each other in the hall and snarl, "Fuck you."

* * *

A fellow was having a few beers at his local pub on a Saturday afternoon when he was approached by a man dressed all in green. "Know what?" the man in green asked confidingly. "I'm a leprechaun, and I'm feeling extremely generous. So generous, in fact, that I'm willing to grant you any three wishes you'd like."

"No kidding! Gee, that's great," blurted the lucky fellow. "I could sure use some extra cash."

"No problem," said the leprechaun with a gracious wave. "The trunk of your car is now crammed with hundred-dollar bills. What's next?"

"Well, I wouldn't mind moving to a nicer house."

"Consider it done," announced the leprechaun grandly. "Four bedrooms, three-and-a-half baths, up on Society Hill. And your third wish?"

"Well, uh, how about a gorgeous blond?" suggested the fellow, blushing a bit.

"She's in your new house, waiting for you in a flimsy negligee."

"This is really great," said the lucky guy, getting down from his stool and starting for the door. "I wish there were some way to thank you."

"Oh, but there is," spoke up the man in green. "I'd like a blow job."

"A blow job?" The man wasn't sure he'd heard right.

"Yup. And after all I've given you, it doesn't seem like much to ask, now does it?"

The lucky fellow had to admit this was true, so in a dark alley behind the bar he obliged his benefactor. As he pulled on his jacket and turned away, the man in green stopped him. "Just one question," he asked. "How old are you?"

"Thirty-four."

"Isn't that a little old to believe in leprechauns?"

* * *

Which doesn't fit with the rest: AIDS, herpes, gonorrhea, condominiums?

Gonorrhea. You can get rid of gonorrhea.

* * *

A cowboy traveling across the desert came across a lovely woman, naked and battered, her limbs tied to four stakes in the ground.

"Thank God you've come!" she cried. "I was on my way to San Francisco when a whole tribe of Indians attacked our wagon train. They stole our food, kidnapped our children, torched our wagons . . . and raped me over and over."

"Lady," said the cowboy as he unbuckled his belt, "today just ain't your day."

* * *

The town gossip came over to the editor of the newspaper and whispered, "Mr. Smith, I do believe I saw Mrs. Smith engaged in carnal relations with someone other than yourself. This was just the other day, underneath that big pine tree in your backyard, you know the one?"

The editor appeared unfazed. "Was the man bald?"

"As a matter of fact he was."

"With a black mustache?"

"I do believe so." The busybody was all atwitter with excitement.

"That's just my chauffeur," said the man with a shrug. "He'll fuck anything."

* * *

How can you tell when a baby's really ugly?

The mother burps it with a hammer.

* * *

Two strangers met on a golf course and the conversation came around to their occupations. The first man said he was in real estate; in fact he owned a condominium complex that could be seen in the distance. The second man said he was a professional assassin, but his new acquaintance was skeptical until the man took some pipes out of his golf bag and assembled them into a rifle.

"I'll be damned," said the first guy.

"The best part of this rifle is the high-power scope," confided the assassin, handing him the gun.

"You're right," said the first man. "I can see inside my apartment with it. There's my wife . . . and she's in there with another man!" Furious, he turned to the assassin and asked how much he charged for his services, to which the reply was, "A thousand dollars a bullet."

The man said, "I want to buy two bullets. I want you to shoot my wife in the head with the first one and blow the guy's balls off with the second."

Agreeing to the offer, the assassin looked through his scope and took aim. Then he lifted his head and said, "If you'll hang on a minute, I can save you a thousand dollars."

* * *

What's the difference between love and herpes?

Herpes is forever.

* * *

Julian finally got Josie to go to bed with him, but after twenty minutes or so of unsatisfying fumbling, he rolled over in frustration and lit up a cigarette.

"What's the matter, Julian?" asked his date. "Can't you think of anyone either?"

* * *

Two Scotsmen were avid golfers and had played together every Thursday for many years. The sixth tee was near the road that led to the local cemetery.

One day as they reached that particular tee a funeral passed by, and old Hamish turned and raised his club in salute.

"Mon," exclaimed Hector, "in all these years we've been a playing this course, and that's the first time I've seen ye pay any attention to someone who's passed away."

"Aye, weel," explained Hamish, "when ye've been married to a woman for forty years, she's entitled to a wee bit of respect."

* * *

"Mom, how do horses have babies?" asked little Dylan one day.

"I don't know," his mother replied. "Your father's a pig."

* * *

The butcher was eager to marry off his only daughter, but to his dismay she showed no interest whatsoever in any of her possible suitors. In fact, she seemed utterly uninterested in sex at all, and her father used to lie awake at night wondering what would become of her.

Late one night, as the butcher headed down to the kitchen for a glass of warm milk, he heard strange sounds coming from his daughter's room. Peering into her room, he saw her masturbating energetically with a hunk of salami.

The next day a customer came into the shop, pointed at the display case, and asked for a half a pound of salami.

"I'm afraid that's not for sale," the butcher told him with a sigh. "That's my son-in-law."

* * *

"Mom, I'm pregnant," announced the sixteen-year-old one morning in a belligerent tone.

Her mother paled.

"And it's all your fault," continued the girl.

"My fault?" gasped her mother, startled. "I bought you books, showed you pictures . . . I told you all about the facts of life."

"Yeah, yeah—but you never taught me how to give a decent blow job, did you?"

* * *

Why's a woman's pussy like a warm toilet seat?

It feels good, but you can't help wondering who was there before you.

* * *

The young lawyer was thrilled to make partner at long last, but disappointed that it didn't immediately make his life easier and more prosperous. In fact, business was hurt by the recession and soon he was bringing home less money that ever. His wife, however, had grown accustomed to a grander vision of their future, and was spending like there was no tomorrow.

Finally he sat down with her to discuss the need to trim their budget a bit. "For starters," he suggested rather snidely, "if you could learn to make something for dinner besides reservations, we could fire the cook."

"That's a thought," she conceded graciously. "And if you'd just learn to fuck, we could fire the gardener."

* * *

What does a man do standing up, a woman do sitting down, and a dog do with one leg raised?

Shake hands.

* * *

Two little kids decide it's time to learn how to swear. The eight-year-old instructs the six-year-old, "Okay, you say 'ass' and I'll say 'hell.'"

All excited about their plan, they troop downstairs, where their mother asks what they want for breakfast. "Aw, hell," says the eight-year-old nonchalantly, "gimme some Cheerios." His mother backhands him off the stool, sends him upstairs bawling, and turns to his brother. "What'll you have?"

"I dunno," quavers the six-year-old, "but you can bet your ass it ain't gonna be Cheerios."

* * *

What's the definition of an anchovy?

A small fish that smells like a finger.

* * *

Laurie fell for her handsome new dentist like a ton of bricks, and pretty soon had lured him into a series of passionate encounters in the dental clinic after hours. But one day he said sadly, "Laurie, honey, we've got to stop seeing each other. Your husband's bound to get suspicious."

"No way, sweetheart, he's dumb as a post," she assured him. "Besides, we've been screwing for six months now and he doesn't suspect a thing."

"True," agreed the dentist, "but you're down to two teeth."

* * *

Know how to keep an asshole in suspense?

I'll tell you later.

* * *

A urologist claimed that he could detect any disease simply by testing the patient's urine, so his pal Joey, who suffered from tennis elbow, decided to pull a prank on him. He made an appointment, received his specimen bottle, and was told to bring it back full the next morning.

That night he peed in the bottle, and so did his wife, his daughter, and the family dog. The next morning Joey jerked off in the bottle to top it off, then innocently handed it over to the receptionist.

Four days went by before the urologist reported back to Joey. "I had a hell of a time with this one," he admitted, "but I think I've got it. Your wife has the clap, your daughter is pregnant, your dog has worms, and if you'd quit jerking off, you wouldn't have tennis elbow."

* * *

Why did the mommy vampire slap the tampon out of her child's hands?

No snacks between meals.

* * *

Three men went out on Sunday to play some golf. On the fourth hole, Fred chipped a shot into the rough. "You all play on ahead," he insisted. "I'll catch up with you."

Off they went, but after half an hour had gone by with no sign of their friend, Charlie said, "I'll go check on him." The last guy played on for a while, but couldn't help wondering what on earth had happened to his companions, so he, too, finally turned back to check matters out.

An astonishing sight greeted him when he returned to the fourth hole: Poor Fred was bent over the back seat of his golf cart, with his buddy energetically screwing him up the ass.

"Charlie, Charlie, what the hell are you doing!" he yelled, breaking into a run.

"It was horrible," gasped a red-faced Charlie. "When I got here, Fred had a massive heart attack."

"You're supposed to give him heart massage, you idiot," cried the third guy, "and mouth-to-mouth resuscitation."

"I know *that*," retorted Charlie indignantly. "How do you think this got started?"

* * *

A Wyoming cowhand went to Denver for a little R&R, but didn't succeed in coping too well with the complexities of city life. In fact, midnight found him alone in his hotel room, jerking off.

Suddenly the door was opened by a bellhop carrying a drink intended for the room next door. "Pardon me, sir," said the flustered bellhop, "but where would you like me to set down your drink?"

"I didn't order a drink," retorted the cowhand, thinking fast. "Can't you see I'm already so drunk that I'm taking advantage of me?"

* * *

What do you call a fight between two test-tube babies?

Jar Wars!

* * *

As a routine part of his examination, the psychiatrist administered a Rorschach test to his newest patient. To his growing dismay, he noted that the young man associated every single ink blot with some sort of extreme sexual perversion. "I'm scheduling you in on Tuesday and Thursday afternoons at three," concluded the doctor firmly. "You need expert professional assistance on a long-term basis."

"Sure, doctor, anything you say," agreed the guy cheerfully, "as long as I can borrow those dirty pictures over the weekend for my big date."

* * *

When Dan's house burned down, his first phone call was to the guy who'd sold him his homeowner's policy. "I need a check for the cash value of my house, and I need it as soon as possible," he said firmly.

"I'm afraid it doesn't work that way," explained the insurance agent politely. "See, yours was a replacement policy, which means that we'll be rebuilding the house exactly as it was before."

"I see," said Dan, after a long pause. "In that case, I want to cancel the policy on my wife."

* * *

The project manager was stuck in a tiny town out in the middle of nowhere, waiting for materials to arrive. One week stretched to two, and by the end of the third week he couldn't take it any more. He went into the local whorehouse, plunked down one hundred dollars, and requested the worst blow job in the joint.

Pocketing the cash, the madam said, "Sir, for one hundred dollars you don't need to settle for the worst. Why, it'll buy you the very best we have to offer."

"Let me set you straight," explained the fellow. "I'm not horny, I'm homesick."

* * *

The very well-dressed man was approached by a shabby, unkempt fellow. "Could you spare a dollar for a cup of coffee?" asked the bum.

"A cup of coffee is only fifty cents," the businessman responded icily.

"Oh I know," replied the bum breezily. "I was hoping you'd join me."

* * *

The saleswoman at the Pink Pussycat boutique didn't bat an eye when the customer purchased an artificial vagina. "What're you going to use it for?" she asked.

"None of your business," answered the customer, thoroughly offended.

"Calm down, buddy," soothed the saleswoman. "The only reason I'm asking is that if it's food, we don't have to charge you sales tax."

* * *

"Mommy, can I swim out to where the waves are breaking?" asked the little girl.

The mother shook her head firmly.

"*Pleeeease?*" she begged. "Daddy's swimming out there."

"I know, darling, but he's insured."

* * *

"Do you talk to your wife while you're having sex?" a man at the bar asked the guy next to him.

He shook his head. "Nope—but I might if I could reach the phone."

* * *

When the wealthy businessman choked on a fish bone at a restaurant, he was fortunate that a surgeon was seated at a nearby table. Springing up, the doctor deftly removed the bone and saved his life.

As soon as the fellow had calmed himself and could talk again, he thanked the surgeon profusely and offered to pay him for his services. "Just name the fee," he croaked gratefully.

"Okay," replied the doctor. "How about half of what you'd have offered when the bone was still stuck in your throat?"

* * *

The train pulled out of Wichita, and the weary businessman was just nodding off when a woman in the upper berth leaned over and said she was cold. Flashing him a winning smile, she asked if he'd mind finding the porter and getting her another blanket.

"Tell you what," proposed the guy. "Why don't we pretend we're married instead?"

"Well . . . okay."

"So we're married. Get your own goddamn blanket!"

* * *

Hear about the young boy whose mother caught him jerking off in the bathroom?

She told him to stop because he'd go blind, and he asked if he could keep going till he needed glasses.

* * *

One night after work, Scott is greeted at the door by his wife clad in a flimsy negligee. Before he has a chance to remove his coat, she falls to her knees, yanks his fly down, pulls his dick out and proceeds to give him a wonderful, sloppy blow job.

"All right!" Scott says. "So what happened to the car?"

* * *

What's the Phone Sex company's motto?

"Reach Out and Touch Someone's."

* * *

Sam was hosting a lavish party to celebrate his thirty lucrative years as a divorce attorney for Hollywood's elite. "You know," he lamented to the friends gathered at his table, "over the years I have donated my legal services to a wide variety of conservation-oriented programs, but am I known as Sam the Environmentalist? No.

"And over the years I have donated hundreds of thousands of dollars to every charity you can imagine, but am I known as Sam the Philanthropist?" His listeners sadly shook their heads.

"But suck one little cock . . . "

* * *

What do sex and bridge have in common?

If you don't have a good partner, a good hand will do.

* * *

Harry and Rachel are celebrating their fiftieth anniversary at the Fontainebleau and it's a hell of a party: champagne, caviar, toasts by all of their best friends assembled for the occasion. Finally, tired and happy, the couple retires to their luxurious suite.

"Rachel," says Harry, "you know this would be the most perfect night of my life if only . . . "

"Oh, Harry," sighs Rachel, "I thought you got over that twenty years ago. You know I don't even like the *idea*."

"But Rachel, darling, it's our fiftieth anniversary. Just this once . . ."

"Harry, you know how I feel about women who do that sort of thing. It's filthy and degrading."

"I know, sweetheart, I know," pleads Harry, "but think how much it'll mean to me."

So Rachel finally gives in, gets up on her knees, and proceeds to go down on her husband. Just as she's finishing, the phone rings. And Harry gets up on one elbow and says, "Answer the phone, cocksucker."

* * *

What's the difference between a drunk and an alcoholic?

Drunks don't have to go to meetings.

* * *

For the four executives, the high point of the annual stockholders meeting was their Sunday afternoon golf game. They had just teed off on the twelfth hole when an assistant golf pro came tearing across the green, red-faced and out of breath. "Mr. Webster, Mr. Webster," he gasped, "I have terrible news. Your wife has just been killed in a car accident."

Webster turned to his companions, and said, "Guys, I gotta warn you. Six more holes and you're gonna see a man crying his eyes out."

* * *

Little Minnie got a real surprise when he barged into his parents' room one night. "And you slap me for sucking my *thumb!*" she screamed.

* * *

What's worse than finding glass in your baby food?

Finding astronaut in your tuna fish.

* * *

A young country girl came to town for a day. She was window shopping when a beautiful pair of red shoes caught her eye, and as she stood admiring them the clerk came out and asked if he could help her. The girl admitted that she'd spent all her money but that she'd do anything to get her hands on those red shoes.

The clerk thought it over for a moment. "I think we can work out a deal," he told her. "Go lie down on the couch in the back room." Soon he came in and closed the door. "So do you want those shoes bad enough to put out for them?" he asked. When she nodded he pulled down his pants, exposing a hard-on nine inches long. "Honey, I'll screw you with this big cock of mine until you squirm and squeal and go wild with desire."

"I don't get much of a kick out of sex, but go right ahead," said the girl, spreading her legs and lying back. Positive she couldn't resist his charms, the salesman started pumping away, but she lay there like a dishrag. Pretty soon he'd come twice and began to worry about getting soft, so he started going at it for all he was worth. Sure enough he felt her arms go around his neck and her legs tighten around his waist. "Best fuck you've ever had, right?" chortled the man. "In a couple of seconds you'll be coming like crazy."

"Oh, no, it's not that," said the girl. "I'm just trying on my new shoes."

* * *

What did one bulldozer say to the other?

"Did the earth move for you, too?"

* * *

A settler in the Dakota wilderness had to protect his family from wild animals and unfriendly Indians—but he also needed to chop wood for the long winter months. So he bought a large bell and set it up outside, instructing his wife to ring it in case of an emergency.

The next day he was chopping away when he heard the bell ring in the distance. Terrified, he grabbed his rifle and ran home, only to find his wife standing in the clearing holding a tray. "I baked you some cookies, honey," she said.

Patiently he explained that the bell was only for a real emergency, and went back to chopping wood. Just a few days later the bell rang again and he rushed back, only to be shown a wounded bird his son had brought home. This, he made clear a little less patiently, was not his idea of a dangerous emergency.

A week later the bell clanged again. Reaching the clearing, the settler found that the house had been felled by a tornado, his wife had been raped and scalped by Indians, and wildcats were gnawing the bloody remains of his children.

"Now, this is more like it!" he declared.

* * *

Why does the crack in your ass go up and down instead of across?

So that when you're sliding downhill, you don't mumble.

* * *

Mr. Jones went to see a sex therapist as a last resort, and confided that his sex life was terrible.

The therapist leaned back in his big leather chair. "I advise having a few martinis first, to loosen things up; then let your mind roam over the whole business of how exciting sex with your wife used to be." The two men glanced out the window, where two dogs happened to be banging away with great abandon in the courtyard. "Now look at the energy and vitality of those two animals," observed the doctor. "Go home, fix a couple of drinks, and think about those spontaneous creatures. Then come back and see me in two weeks."

Two weeks later the therapist asked, "Well, how did it go?"

"Terrible," moaned Jones. "It took seven martinis just to get her out in the yard."

* * *

What happens when you cross a prostitute with a computer?

You get a fucking know-it-all.

* * *

One night Judge O'Brien tottered into his house very late and very drunk, indeed so bombed that he had thrown up all over himself. In the morning he sheepishly told his wife that a drunk sitting next to him on the train home had managed to vomit on him.

The judge made it into the courthouse, where it occurred to him that his story might not be truly convincing. Inspired, he called home and said, "Marge, you won't believe this, but the drunk who threw up on me last night just showed up in court, and I gave him thirty days."

"Give him sixty," said the judge's wife. "He shat in your pants, too."

* * *

What did Raggedy Anne say as she was sitting on Pinocchio's face?

"Tell the truth! Tell a lie! Tell the truth! Tell a lie!"

* * *

Jerry had gone in for a routine checkup, and when he came back in for the results his doctor sounded very solemn indeed. "I think you'd better sit down, Jerry. I've got some good news and some bad news."

Jerry steeled himself. "Give me the bad news."

"You've got cancer. It's metastasized widely, it's spreading unbelievably fast, it's totally inoperable, and you've got a month or less left."

"Jesus Christ," gasped Jerry, wiping the cold sweat off his forehead. "What the hell's the good news?"

"You know that really cute new receptionist out in the front office?" asked the doctor.

"Sure do," answered Jerry.

"The one with the big tits and that adorable ass?"

"Yup."

"And the long, gorgeous blond hair?"

"Yeah, yeah," said Jerry impatiently.

"Well," said the doctor, leaning forward with a grin, "I'm screwing her!"

* * *

It's after dinner when this guy realizes he's out of cigarettes. He decides to pop down to the corner bar for a pack, telling his wife he'll be right back. The bartender offers him a draft on the house and he decides he has time for just one. He's nursing it when a gorgeous blond comes in the door, but he looks the other way because he knows he has no time to fool around. Can he help it if she comes and sits right next to him and says how thirsty she is?

One thing leads to another and eventually the girl says how much she likes him and invites him back to her apartment to get better acquainted. How can he refuse? Back at her place they go at it like crazy, and the next thing he knows it's four o'clock in the morning. Jumping out of bed, the guy shakes the girl awake and asks if she has any baby powder.

"Yeah, in the bathroom cabinet," she says groggily.

He dusts his hands liberally, drives home at ninety mph, and pulls into the driveway to find his wife waiting up for him with a rolling pin in her hand. "So where've you been?" she screeches.

"Well, you see, honey," he stammers, "I only went out for cigarettes, but Jake offered me a beer and then this beautiful bombshell walked in and we got to talking and drinking and we've been back at her apartment fucking like bunnies . . . "

"Wait a minute," snaps his wife. "Let me see your hands." Turning on him furiously, she says, "Don't you *ever* try lying to me again, you rotten little skunk—you've been bowling again!"

* * *

A rather scruffy-looking type came into a bank. Reaching the head of the line, he said to the teller, "I wanna open a fucking checking account."

"Certainly, sir," answered the teller, "but there's no need to use that kind of language."

"Couldja move it along lady? I just wanna open a fucking checking account," growled the would-be customer.

"I'll be glad to be of service, sir," said the teller, flushing slightly, "but I would appreciate not being spoken to in that way."

"Just lemme open a fucking checking account, okay?"

"I'm afraid I'm going to have to speak to the branch manager," said the flustered teller, slipping off her stool and returning shortly with a dapper middle-aged man who asked how he could be of service.

"I just won the ten-million dollar lottery, buddy," snarled the man, "and all I wanna do is open a fucking checking account."

"I see," said the manager sympathetically. "And this bitch is giving you trouble?"

* * *

Then there are the two versions of the Little Red Riding Hood story:

Once upon a time there was a little girl named Little Red Riding Hood. One fine morning she set out for Grandma's house, putting a freshly baked cake and a .357 Magnum in her basket. And what should she find when she got to Grandma's but a big bad wolf in the bed. The ferocious beast grabbed the girl, shredded her dress, and snarled, "I'm going to bang you till the cows come home."

"Oh no you're not," retorted Little Red Riding Hood, pulling out the gun. "You're going to eat me like the story says."

or

Once upon a time there was a little girl called Little Red Riding Hood. One fine morning she set out for Grandma's house with a freshly baked cake in her basket. And what should she find when she reached her grandmother's but a big bad wolf hiding in the bed. The beast jumped up, grabbed the girl, and snarled, "You've had it, little girl—I'm going to eat you right up."

"Eat, eat, eat," sighed Little Red Riding Hood. "Doesn't anyone fuck anymore?"

* * *

Little Jason came up to his father at the breakfast table one morning and declared, "Daddy, when I grow up, I want to be just like you."

"Aw, son, that makes me feel great," said his Dad, patting him on the head. "I'd love to have an engineer for a son."

"That's not what I mean, Daddy," said Jason. "I mean I want to fuck Mommy."

* * *

Especially horny one night, Sam rolled over and nuzzled his wife. "How about it, honey?" he asked tenderly.

"Oh, Sam, I've got an appointment with the gynecologist tomorrow," said his wife, going on to explain that the doctor had requested that she abstain from intercourse for twenty-four hours before an appointment.

Sam sighed deeply and turned over to his side of the bed. A few minutes later he rolled back and asked hopefully, "You don't have a dentist appointment too, do you?"

* * *

An attorney was defending a man accused of first-degree murder. "Your Honor," he began, "my client is accused of stuffing his lover's mutilated body into a suitcase and heading for the Mexican border. Just north of Tijuana, a cop spotted her hand sticking out of the suitcase.

"Now I would like to stress that my client is *not* a murderer. A sloppy packer, maybe . . . "

* * *

Six-year old Teddy came into the house with his hands cupped together and asked, "Mom, is there such a thing as boy grasshoppers?"

"Why, yes, honey. Why do you ask?"

"How about girl grasshoppers?" persisted Teddy.

Not ready to deal with the whole issues of the birds and the bees with her innocent little boy, Mrs. Englehardt patted him on the head and answered, "No, dear."

170

"Just wondering," said Teddy, smiling sweetly. Turning away, he clapped his hands together and screamed, "FAGGOTS!"

* * *

How do married couples do it doggie-style?

Without all the licking and sniffing.

* * *

A young woman was sitting on the bus cooing to her baby when a drunk staggered aboard and down the aisle. Stopping in front of her, he looked down and pronounced, "Lady, that is the ugliest baby I have ever seen."

The woman burst into tears, and there was such an outcry of sympathy among the other passengers that they kicked the drunk off. But the woman kept on sobbing and wailing, so loudly that finally the driver pulled the bus over to the side of the road.

"Look, I don't know what that bum said to you," the driver told his inconsolable passenger, "but to help calm you down I'm going to get you a cup of tea." And off he went, coming back shortly with a cup of tea from the corner deli.

"Now calm down, lady," soothed the driver, "everything's going to be okay. See, I brought you a cup of nice, hot tea, and I even got a banana for your monkey."

* * *

Define "egghead":

What Mrs. Dumpty gives to Humpty.

* * *

What do a blow job and Eggs Benedict have in common?

They're the only two things you never get at home.

* * *

When Ross showed up for his appointment with the urologist, the doctor informed him a sperm sample was necessary, and instructed him to go to Room Four. Dutifully heading for Room Four, Ross found two absolutely gorgeous women clad in scanty lingerie. They proceeded to arouse him beyond his wildest dreams, and Ross headed back down the hall with a dreamy smile and a *terrific* sperm sample.

Realizing he had to pee, Ross opened the door to the first bathroom he came across, only to interrupt a guy frantically beating off with a copy of *Hustler*. In the second bathroom a fellow was busy masturbating with the company of the *Penthouse* centerfold.

Back in the doctor's office and curious as hell, Ross couldn't resist asking the doctor about the other two fellows.

"Oh, those guys?" asked the doctor dismissively. "Those're my Medicaid patients."

* * *

When Alec was informed by his doctor that he had only twelve more hours to live, he rushed home and told his wife, who collapsed in racking sobs. But then she pulled herself together, clasped his hands in hers, and promised, "Then I'm going to make tonight the best night of your life, darling." She went out and bought all his favorite delicacies, opened a bottle of fine champagne, served him dinner dressed in his favorite sexy peignoir, and led him up to bed, where she made passionate love to him.

Just as they were about to fall asleep, Alec tapped her on the shoulder. "Honey, could we do it again?"

"Sure, sweetheart," she said sleepily.

"Once more, baby?" he asked afterwards. "It's our last night together."

"Mmmhmm," she mumbled, and they made love a third time.

"One last time, darling," he begged a little later, shaking her by the shoulders.

"Fine!" she snapped. "After all, what do you care? *You* don't have to get up in the morning."

* * *

What's the difference between your paycheck and your wife?

You don't have to beg your wife to blow your paycheck.

* * *

The psychiatrist closed his notebook, clasped his hands in satisfaction, and contemplated the patient sitting across from him. "I confess that in my profession one seldom speaks of 'cures,' Miss Kamin," he said sagely, "but at this time I am very pleased to be able to pronounce you one hundred percent cured. Good-bye, and good luck."

"Swell," muttered the woman, looking downcast and beginning to pout. "That's just swell."

The psychiatrist was taken by surprise. "Miss Kamin, I thought you'd be delighted. What on earth is wrong?"

"Oh, it's fine for you," she snapped, "but look at it from my side. Three years ago I was Joan of Arc. Now I'm nobody."

* * *

"Tell me the truth, Doctor Hill," said the emaciated fellow. "How much longer am I going to live?"

"It's always hard to predict," she replied brightly, "but let's just say that if I were you, I wouldn't start watching any miniseries on TV."

* * *

An amateur golfer playing in his first tournament was delighted when a beautiful girl came up to him after the round and suggested he come over to her place for a while. The fellow was a bit embarrassed to explain that he really couldn't stay all night but that he'd be glad to come over for a while. Twenty minutes later they were in her bed making love. And when it was over, he got out of bed and started getting dressed.

"Hey," called the girl from beneath the covers, "where do you think you're going? Arnold Palmer wouldn't leave so early."

At that the golfer stripped off his clothes and jumped on top of her. Once they'd made love a second time, he got out of bed and put his pants back on.

"What're you up to?" she called out. "Jack Nicklaus wouldn't think of leaving now." So the golfer pulled off his pants and screwed her a third time, and afterwards he started getting dressed.

"C'mon, you can't leave yet," protested the girl. "Lee Trevino wouldn't call it a day."

"Lady, would you tell me one thing?" asked the golfer, looking at her very seriously. "What's par for this hole?"

* * *

When do you know you're really lonely?

When your own tongue starts to feel good in your mouth.

* * *

The hooker came up to the single man at the bar and said boldly, "I cost three hundred dollars—and I'm worth it."

"Is that so?" asked the fellow, looking her over. "Three hundred bucks is a lot of money."

Snuggling up so that he could smell her perfume and leaning over so he could appreciate her cleavage, the hooker proceeded to elaborate upon the skills, the techniques, the talent and imagination she brought to her trade. "I'll make love to you like you've never been made love to before," she promised throatily. "In fact, whisper any three words—picture your wildest fantasy coming true—and I'll make it happen."

"Any three words? For three hundred dollars?" he asked, perking up considerably.

"That's right, baby," confirmed the prostitute, blowing him a pouty little kiss.

"You've got a deal." The man pulled her up onto his lap, ran his hand up under her skirt, pulled her long blond hair away from her ear, and whispered, "Paint my house."

* * *

What's the worst thing about our jury trial system?

You're leaving your fate in the hands of twelve people too stupid to get out of jury duty.

TOO TASTELESS TO BE INCLUDED

How do you make a woman scream twice?
　　Fuck her up the ass, then wipe it on the curtain.

* * *

Why do husbands abuse their wives?
　　Why not?

* * *

Why are babies born with soft spots on top of their heads?
　　So that if there's a fire in the hospital, the nurse can carry out five with each hand.

* * *

Did you hear about the fellow who chewed his baby's toes off?
　　He forgot his wife was pregnant.

* * *

Two fanatical fisherman were accustomed to fishing alongside one another in companionable silence every weekend, no matter what the weather or the season. Then, one weekend, one of them failed to appear. Nor did he show the next weekend. But on the third Saturday he was back in his usual spot.

　　"Missed you," said the first fisherman after an hour or so had passed.

　　"Got married."

　　Half an hour later the first one said, "She must be something to keep you off fishing for two weekends. Is she that gorgeous?"

　　"Nothing special," said the newlywed.

　　Half an hour later the first man spoke up again. "She a good cook?"

　　"If you like frozen food."

In due course came the next question. "She must be dynamite in bed then, eh?"

"Same as all the rest," said the second fisherman, shrugging offhandedly.

"So why'd you marry her?" demanded the first, unable to contain his curiosity.

"She's got worms."

* * *

What's grosser than gross?

When a girl is giving you a blow job in the back seat of the car and somebody crashes into you.

What's grosser than that?

When somebody slaps her on the back!

* * *

"Honey, I think the twins got into the rat poison."

"That's okay—they'll crawl under the house to die."

* * *

Why do farts smell?

So blind people can appreciate them, too.

* * *

Why don't black women let their toddlers play in the sandbox?

Because cats keep trying to bury them.

* * *

What's red and crawls up your leg?

A homesick abortion.

* * *

What's grosser than gross?

Finding a pubic hair in your Bloody Mary.

Even grosser?

Biting into your hot dog and finding veins in it.

Even grosser?

Screwing a pregnant woman and the fetus gives you head.

* * *

When his girlfriend died suddenly, Jimmy was truly distraught. When the truck came to take her off to the morgue, he pulled the attendant aside and asked if he could pay a final visit to his beloved.

"Sure," said the guy, but indicated it would cost him.

Jimmy readily agreed, handed over the money at the morgue, and was shown to the room where her corpse lay on an autopsy table. "God, I'd really like to kiss her one more time," he admitted wistfully. The attendant named a price, and though he was getting short on cash, Jimmy readily handed it over.

After the kiss, Jimmy looked up with tears in his eyes and confessed that he still found her incredibly attractive, so much so that he desperately wanted to do it with her one more time.

Nervous about someone coming in, the attendant finally agreed that in return for the last of Jimmy's cash, he would cut out the relevant part of the woman's anatomy and hand it over. "Would you like it wrapped up?" he asked.

"No, thank you," answered Jimmy. "I'll eat it here."

* * *

Why do German shower heads have eleven holes?

Because Jews only have ten fingers.

* * *

Do you know why Hitler committed suicide?

He got the gas bill.

* * *

How do you make Instant Easter?

Two boards and a Jew.

* * *

Have you heard about Tempura House?

It's the new halfway house for lightly battered women.

* * *

What goes "hop, skip, jump, ka-blam!"?

Nicaraguan children playing in a mine field.

* * *

Why are African-Americans so quick on their feet?

Because they spend their first nine months dodging coat hangers.

* * *

What's the best thing about having a homeless shelter in the neighborhood?

It keeps the flies away from your place.

* * *

Did you hear about the Puerto Rican who didn't know the difference between arson and incest?

He set his sister on fire.

* * *

How can you tell when your kid's in a tough school?

They do abortions in biology lab.

* * *

What do inner-city mothers use instead of a crib?

A dumpster.

* * *

How does a West Virginian mom know when her daughter has her period?

Her son tastes funny.

* * *

How can you tell your son's being abused at his day-care center?

He won't use a pacifier unless it's got hair on it.

How can you tell your daughter's being abused at her day-care center?

You hand her a broom and she straddles it.

* * *

Two women were waiting their turn at the abortion clinic, and one couldn't help noticing the other was furiously knitting away at what looked like a little bonnet. Finally she couldn't restrain herself. "I know it's none of my business," she said, "but how can you have the heart to sit there knitting a baby bonnet when you're about to have an abortion?"

"Oh, it's not a bonnet," said the other woman matter-of-factly. "It's a body bag."